JELLIES, JAMS & CHUTNEYS

JELLIES, JAMS & CHUTNEYS

PRESERVING THE HARVEST

THANE PRINCE

DK

London New York Munich
Melbourne Delhi

Food photography by Jean Cazals

Project Editor Diana Craig
Designer Carole Ash at Project 360
Editor Siobhán O'Connor
Location photographer Steve Lee
Food Stylist Katie Rogers
Props Stylist Sue Rowlands

Senior Art Editor Susan Downing
Project Editors Anna Davidson and
Laura Nickoll
US Editor Anja Schmidt
Managing Editor Dawn Henderson
Production Editor Ben Marcus
Production Controller Wendy Penn

First American edition, 2008
Published in the United States by
DK Publishing, 375 Hudson Street,
New York, New York 10014

07 08 09 10 11   10 9 8 7 6 5 4 3 2 1

JD072–2008

Published in Great Britain
by Dorling Kindersley Limited

A catalog record for this book is available
from the Library of Congress

ISBN: 978-0-7566-3691-3

DK books are available at special discounts
when purchased in bulk for sales promotions,
premiums, fund-raising, or educational use. For
details, contact: DK Publishing Special Markets,
375 Hudson Street, New York, New York 10014
or SpecialSales@dk.com

Color reproduction by Colourscan, Singapore
Printed and bound by Leo Paper Products Ltd, China

Discover more at **www.dk.com**

Contents

6 Introduction

8 Techniques

24 Summer berries

50 Stone fruit

74 Summer vegetables

108 Orchard fruit

130 Flowers and herbs

146 Wild harvest

162 Tropical fruit

180 Chiles and spices

200 Winter citrus

220 Index

224 Acknowledgments

Introduction

What is it about making preserves that so entrances me? It isn't my sweet tooth, as my consumption often lags far behind my production levels. Nor is it, with so many wonderful farmers' markets and specialty shops around, all selling jams, jellies, and pickles of every kind, a void on my pantry shelf that needs to be filled. I think the answer is that standing in my kitchen stirring a pan of steaming fruit or vegetables, then ladling the resulting mixture into jars, is a truly life-enhancing experience. It links me to all those cooks of the past for whom preserving nature's bounty was a necessity, rather than an indulgence. There is also the pride that one feels when looking at a jewel-bright row of homemade jellies on the pantry shelf. And there is joy, too, when offering a dish of brilliant red raspberry jam to a friend or contributing a jar to the local fundraiser, in being able to say: "This? I made it myself."

The really good news about making preserves at home is that, while it might at first appear to be a complex art, it is wonderfully simple once a few basic rules have been understood. Most recipes are well within the reach of the novice cook. For me, the first rule is to ask myself: "Is this truly worth preserving?" Although I like to feel virtuous, I do not wish to have shelf after shelf filled with jars of zucchini pickles made—let's be honest—with huge, overblown squash. Whether you buy from the farmers' market or harvest from your own vegetable patch, preserve only the freshest and best of the crop. In the case of chutneys, ketchups, and sauces, there is a little leeway, as here you can use just-overripe tomatoes, plums, etc.; for jams, jellies, and pickles, however, only the finest quality fruits and vegetables will do. Making your own preserves will lend a seasonal quality to your cooking. Beginning with spring's elderflowers, you can traverse the year, filling jars with the first fruits of summer, as well as the last ones of autumn. Even when winter has you in its icy grip, a simmering pot of pickled dried figs or the vibrancy of cranberry vodka can cheer a cook's day.

Another aspect of preserve making that can seem confusing is the terminology. When is a jam not a jam, but a conserve? In this book, I've used the term "jam" when the fruit tends to break down during cooking, "preserve" when there are large chunks of fruit, and "conserve" when the fruits remain whole. This is only a rough guide, and you will no doubt find inconsistencies, as some jams simply cry

out to be called preserves, while occasionally conserve seems to be the name of choice. Pickles, on the other hand, are more clearly defined. A pickle is a vegetable or fruit preserve that is essentially raw, preserved in spiced vinegar. Pickles have nowhere to hide in their clear vinegar-filled jars, so the vegetables used must always be of the finest quality, without blemish or bruise. Making chutneys is to my mind one of life's great pleasures. From chopping the onions and grating the ginger to simmering the rich and fragrant mixture, making a large pot of chutney can lift the lowest of spirits. But a word of caution here: don't leave the pot unattended while it simmers, as there is a real tendency for the chutney to scorch—often just at the moment it's ready. Burnt chutney enhances no one's life. Finally, flavoring your own spirits and making your own liqueurs is simplicity itself. Buy good-quality vodka or gin, and use top-quality fragrant fruits. I store most of these liqueurs in the freezer, where they develop a pleasant consistency, and the cold enhances the rather sweet flavor. Serve these homemade liqueurs in your smallest, prettiest glasses—then sit back to enjoy the compliments.

Whether you are new to the kitchen or an experienced cook, I hope you will find here recipes that spark memories of meals eaten when young, some hint of holidays in exotic locations, and new ideas that tempt you into the kitchen, to chop, grate, and slice your way to the perfect preserve.

Thane Prince

Techniques

Equipment • Sterilizing and potting • Understanding pectin
Making jams, jellies, curds, and cheeses
Making chutneys and relishes • Brining, salting, and pickling

Equipment

Much of the equipment needed to make preserves will probably already be part of your kitchen armory, but there are a few specialty items you may require, depending on what you want to make. Check out the preserve-maker's kit that is listed here, and buy or borrow additional equipment as necessary.

Preparing and cooking

PRESERVING POT

The best pot to use is one that is wider than it is deep. This conducts heat quickly, so that the jam or jelly reduces fast, retaining its fresh flavor, and boils rapidly, which enables it to achieve a set. For chutneys and relishes, it is important that the pot also has a heavy base to achieve an even heat. Go for stainless-steel or enameled pans, avoiding aluminum, as this reacts with the acids in fruit and vinegar. Preserving pots are available from kitchen shops and mail-order outlets, or you can improvise. I use an enameled cast-iron casserole 12in (30cm) wide and 6in (15cm) deep.

JELLY BAGS AND STAND

A jelly bag stand and two or three jelly bags (see p18) are a good investment, or improvise by dripping the juice through a fine-woven cloth such as butter muslin, a fine sieve lined with a double-thickness of cheesecloth, or a clean old dish towel, hung between the upended legs of a

PRESERVING POT

JAM FUNNEL

GRATERS AND SIEVES

SPOONS

stool. Wash and scald bags, muslin, cheesecloth, and dish towels before use. When dry, press with a hot iron to sterilize.

MEASURING EQUIPMENT
• Scales for accurate weighing of fruit, vegetables, and sugar.
• 1 quart measuring cup and a 2 cup measuring jug (optional).
• Spoon measures for accurate weighing of spices, etc.

GRATERS AND SIEVES
• Microplane or similar grater for ginger, garlic, and zest.

• A food mill, such as a mouli, for grating vegetables.
• Sieve to remove seeds from jam, if desired.

SPOONS
• Large slotted spoon for removing scum.
• Wooden spoons for stirring and for the flake test (see p17).
• Metal spoons for tasting, etc.

JAM FUNNEL
Try to find a wide-mouthed funnel, as this will make it easier to fill the jars.

Potting

CONTAINERS

Jars must be scrupulously clean and sterilized before use. A dishwasher set on hot fulfills both these requirements, so running the jars through the machine to be ready when the jam is due to be potted is a good idea. Alternatively, wash the jars in hot, soapy water, rinse well, then drain until nearly dry. Put in a cold oven and heat at 300°F (150°C) for 10–15 minutes. Olive oil and vinegar bottles, well washed, dried, and sealed with a lined screwtop or cork lid, are good for flavored vinegars. Pretty bottles with hinged glass tops and rubber seals, available from hardware stores and canning suppliers, are excellent for all vinegars, sauces, and liqueurs.

COVERS

Lids with vinegar-proof inner plastic or rubber rings are the best all-around covers, and there is no need to use waxed paper circles. Lids with no inner rings may be used for vinegar-free preserves, or jars can be sealed with cellophane covers. Dip each cover in water. Place, damp side down, over the jar. Stretch the cellophane tightly, holding it in place with a rubber band. In both cases, top the preserve with a waxed paper circle first, cut to fit the top of the jar. Place this directly on the hot preserve, then screw on the lid or stretch over the cellophane cover.

INNER PLASTIC OR RUBBER RINGS must be used to seal chutneys and pickles.

EXISTING LIDS may be used, provided that they show no signs of rust or other deterioration.

CELLOPHANE COVERS, stretched over jars, will tighten as the jam cools.

GLASS CONTAINERS without chips or cracks can be recycled to use for potting preserves.

Potting jams and chutneys

It's worth taking a little time to consider how you will package your preserves. The size and shape of the jar you use depends on the preserve it will contain. Breakfast marmalade is fine in a large, plain pot, but jellies and pickles to give as gifts will look better in small, interestingly shaped jars. I like to save pretty jars to keep for future use.

How to pot sweet preserves

Once you decide that your jam or jelly has reached the setting point, you need to ladle it into a jar while the preserve is still hot.

1 GETTING READY
Have ready hot clean sterilized jars, clean sterilized lids (if using), a spotlessly clean jam funnel, and a ladle or large metal spoon. Position the jars on a baking tray or heatproof surface, close to the pan to minimize spills.

2 FILLING THE JARS
Set the funnel over the first jar and ladle the preserve into it, allowing the preserve to fill the jar to within ½in (1cm) of the top. Take care to try not to dribble the preserve around the top of the jar.

3 SEALING THE JARS
If using wax discs (see p11), place these on top of the hot jam at once, then cover with the cellophane jam covers, if using. If you are using lids, place them loosely on the hot jars, and tighten later once the jars are cool.

FILLING THE JARS

SEALING THE JARS

Microwaving jam

Microwave jams are simple and fun. Thinner than those made on a stove, they must be stored in the refrigerator, but are quickly made. The basic principle of microwave jam is to take 1lb 2oz (500g) of prepared fruit and 12oz (350g) sugar, plus the juice of a lemon. Put in a deep glass bowl with a capacity of at least 8 cups. Microwave on high for 2- to 3-minute intervals, stirring often, until the setting point is reached. To test, put a spoonful of jam on a cold plate and allow to cool. When thick enough, ladle into sterilized jars, and store in the refrigerator.

How to pot savory preserves

The only key difference between potting sweet preserves and savory ones is that the latter require vinegar-proof lids.

1 GETTING READY
Have ready hot sterilized jars with vinegar-proof lids (see p11), a jam funnel, and a ladle or large metal spoon. Place these on a baking tray or heatproof surface near the preserving pan.

2 FILLING THE JARS
Using the jam funnel, spoon the hot preserve into the jars, leaving about ½–¾in (1–2cm) head space. If a chutney or relish is very thick or chunky, it is sometimes necessary to use a spoon to pack the mixture down into the jars to avoid air gaps. I use a clean metal teaspoon to do this.

3 SEALING THE JARS
Once the jar is filled, screw on the lids, or close them in the case of hinged lids. You may need to tighten screwtop lids again once the jars have cooled, to create a proper seal.

Storing your preserves

• **Labeling** Be sure to label your jars clearly, both with the name of the preserve and the date when it was potted. I always think I'll remember what is in which jar, but chutneys can look remarkably like jam!
• **Where to store** Unless otherwise stated, store all preserves in a cool, dark cupboard or pantry. Once opened, store in the refrigerator and use within the stated time.

Heat processing

The water-bath or heat processing method offers additional protection against contamination by molds or bacteria. Cellophane-covered jars are not suitable.

• **Filling the pan** You need a special water-canner or a large lidded saucepan into which you can fit a rack at the bottom. Put the pan on the burner, and half-fill with boiling water. Set the filled and tightly sealed jars on the rack so that they are close but not touching. Resting on the rack, the jars are protected from the direct heat source beneath. Add more boiling water until the jars are submerged by ¾–1in (2–2.5cm).
• **Boiling the jars** Cover the pan with a lid, bring the water to a boil, and, once boiling, start timing. Process the jars for 10–15 minutes at 185°F (85°C) for sweet preserves and 212°F (100°C) for savory.
• **Storing the jars** Remove the jars using tongs, and allow to cool before storing in a cool, dark place. For further information, consult the US Department of Agriculture website. Please note this method is for processing preserves only, and not for canning raw fruits and vegetables.

Making sweet preserves

A shelf lined with jams and jellies, brightly colored and full of promise, is easily within even the most modest cook's grasp. Homemade jam has a freshness with which store-bought alternatives cannot compete, so get out your largest pan and get cooking.

Ingredients for sweet preserves

FRUIT AND VEGETABLES

Always use best-quality fruits and vegetables—it is pointless preserving anything second-rate. They should be firm, just ripe, and without blemishes. Try to make your preserves as soon as possible after the fruit and vegetables are picked, and make sure everything is clean and grit-free. Hand-picked berries can be sorted and, if very soft and dust-free (such as raspberries), won't need washing. Strawberries, red currants, etc., should be rinsed under cold running water; rinse more robust fruit under warm water. A good scrub in cold water cleans most vegetables that aren't being peeled. To remove the wax coating on store-bought fruit such as some apples and most citrus, scrub the fruit in hot water with a plastic scouring pad.

SUGAR

For a good set, you need the correct quantities of sugar, pectin, and acid. White granulated sugar gives as good a result as more expensive preserving sugars. Raw sugar (light and dark muscovado, molasses, Demerara, and golden granulated) can be used, but make the jam darker and can mask the fruit's fresh flavor. An exception is dark full-flavored marmalade: here, I always opt for raw sugar. When making marmalade with sweet oranges, I use sugar with added pectin. The ratio of sugar to acid and pectin allows a set, so sugar must be carefully weighed. It must also be completely dissolved before the jam or jelly is boiled, so stir over a low heat until no grittiness remains, then increase to a full rolling boil (see p16).

Understanding pectin

• With commercial pectin, the amount needed is in direct ratio to the amount of sugar used. The correct quantity will be marked on the box or bottle, so follow the manufacturer's instructions.

• Make your own pectin by puréeing leftover lemon shells with water. Boil the mixture in a nonreactive saucepan, then let the juices drip through a jelly bag (see p208). Use within 2 days.

• Adding fruit that is high in pectin to fruit that lacks enough is another way to achieve a good set in your jam or jelly. Apples, red currants, and gooseberries are all pectin-rich.

PECTIN

When combined with sugar and acid, pectin—which is a naturally occurring soluble fiber—forms a bond that causes jam to set. Fruits vary in their pectin content; if a fruit is low in this fiber, it needs to be boiled for a long time to achieve the right concentration of pectin. Adding extra pectin allows for a shorter boiling time and thus a fresher-tasting jam. You can add extra pectin in three ways: with commercial pectin, by making your own (see above), or by adding fruits high in pectin to a jam or jelly being made with fruits that are low in pectin. Commercial pectin is available in liquid or powder form. I have used liquid pectin in this book for convenience, but powdered pectin works equally well.

ACID

Acidity is the final concern when making sweet preserves. This is quite simple: does the fruit taste roughly as acidic as lemon juice? For example, gooseberries, raspberries, currants, and cooking apples when boiled all taste very acidic. If the fruit does not have that sharp tang, you will need to acidify it further. The simplest way is to add freshly squeezed lemon juice. Juice from other high-acid fruit can also be used, with red currant juice being the most common. Powdered citric or tartaric acid is another option: 1 teaspoon powder in 1¾fl oz (50ml) water is the equivalent of 2 tablespoons lemon juice. Adding currant, sour apple, or gooseberry juice can supply both the acid and pectin needed.

How to make jam

Cooking jam involves first cooking the fruit, then boiling the mixture until it reaches the setting point. Depending on the fruit used, sugar is added at various stages.

1 COOKING THE FRUIT

Cook the fruit gently, with or without sugar. With delicate fruits, such as raspberries, add the sugar at the start of cooking. For tougher or thicker-skinned fruits, such as blueberries, black currants, cranberries, and citrus, you must boil the fruit or peel first to soften it, then add the sugar and cook until the sugar has dissolved. Add pectin and acid (lemon juice), if using, according to the method.

2 RAPID BOILING

Increase the heat and bring the mixture to a "full rolling boil." You can tell when your jam has reached this point because it will be boiling so hard that you will not be able to stir the bubbles down with a wooden spoon. Boil the mixture hard for the required time, so that the pectin interacts with the sugar to achieve a set.

3 SKIMMING

Skim off any scum as it rises to the surface (see p18). When skimming marmalade, make sure you do so as soon as the mixture begins to boil; otherwise the scum will bond with the peel later, once the jars are cool.

4 TESTING FOR A SET

Study your jam: as it reaches the setting point, the mixture will begin to thicken a little around the sides of the pan, will boil more sluggishly, and the bubbles will "plop," rather than froth. I find that the best method is to test once after 3–5 minutes of boiling, then every 2–3 minutes until a set is shown. Always turn off the heat while you test the jam.

RAPID BOILING

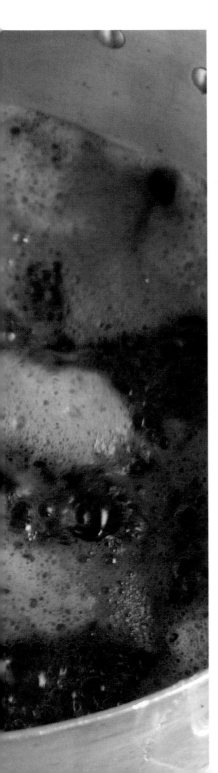

The flake test Using a clean wooden spoon, scoop up a small amount of jam. Allow it to cool for a moment, then gently tilt the spoon to pour the jam back into the pot. If the final part of the jam falls in a flake, rather than a stream, the jam is ready.

The wrinkle test Keep a supply of plates in the refrigerator or freezer. Take a cold plate and spoon on about 1 teaspoon of jam. Allow the jam to cool, then push it from the side with your finger. If the surface of the jam wrinkles, it is ready.

How to make jellies

Jellies are made from the strained juice of the fruit, which is cooked first, strained through a jelly bag, and the pulp discarded.

1 COOKING THE FRUIT
Simmer the fruit in water, without any sugar, until it is soft.

2 STRAINING THE FRUIT
Allow the resulting pulp to drip through a scalded jelly bag, piece of muslin, or dish towel for at least 12 hours, to extract all the juice. Do not be tempted to squeeze the bag, as this will cause the jelly to be cloudy.

3 ADDING THE SUGAR
Measure the juice and add the sugar, usually in the ratio of 1lb (450g) sugar to each 2 cups liquid, or according to the recipe.

4 BOILING AND SKIMMING
Bring to a full rolling boil, as for jam (see p16), skimming off any scum. The simplest method is to use a shallow slotted spoon, and a bowl of warm water. Carefully skim the scum from the surface of the mixture, then dip the spoon into the water each time to ensure a clean finish. Take care not to stir the scum down into the mixture. If you are adding flowers, chopped herbs, or seeds, it is best to do so after skimming.

5 TESTING FOR A SET
Test for a set using either the flake test or the wrinkle test (see p17).

STRAINING THE FRUIT

BOILING AND SKIMMING

SIEVING THE MIXTURE

How to make curds, butters, and cheeses

Traditionally, fruit curds always incorporate dairy products and eggs, while fruit butters and fruit cheeses have no dairy products. Fruit cheeses were originally always potted into molds, then turned out and sliced.

1 SIEVING THE MIXTURE
As the fruit is not usually peeled when making fruit butters and cheeses, the mixture is sieved to remove the peel and seeds.

2 TESTING FOR A SET
With fruit curd, cook the mixture without boiling, stirring constantly, until it coats the back of a spoon. The curd will continue to thicken as it cools. To test fruit butter, spread a little on a plate; if no rim of liquid appears around the edge of the mixture, the fruit butter is ready. Test fruit cheese by drawing a spoon across the bottom of the pan: it should leave a clear line through the fruit cheese.

3 POURING INTO A MOLD
If you wish to use your fruit butter or cheese at once, it can be set in a mold when it has reached setting point, then sliced and served.

POURING INTO A MOLD

How to make vinegars, cordials, and drinks

Many fruits and herbs can be used to make vinegars, cordials, and flavored alcohols. You need to choose good-quality flavorings, so go for ripe fruit, fresh bright herbs, and freshly ground or crushed spices. Vinegars and alcohols, on the other hand, should be of high quality but bland taste. I use white wine vinegar of at least 6 percent alcohol content for vinegars, and vodka for liqueurs.

Making savory preserves

Savory preserves such as chutneys and pickles don't have the immediacy of jams and jellies, as maturing the mix is often necessary for optimum taste. I love making them, all the while thinking of the promise of good things to come lined up in the pantry.

Ingredients for savory preserves

FRUIT AND VEGETABLES

For chutneys, relishes, ketchups, and sauces, you can use slightly overripe and even some less than perfect specimens, as long as you cut out and discard any bruised or damaged parts. Pickles, though, need the best-quality ingredients: they will not be cooked for a long period, if at all, so the freshness of the ingredients must always shine through. As with making jams and jellies, you need to scrub off the wax coating on any store-bought fruit that has been treated in this way before using it in any of your preserves.

SUGAR

I usually use a raw sugar such as muscovado for chutneys, as it gives a wonderfully deep flavor and color. Fresher-tasting relishes are better made with white granulated or light unrefined sugars such as Demerara. Muscovado sugar is available in three main types: light, dark, and molasses. These types vary according to the amount of raw molasses that is left in the sugar. For most chutneys, light muscovado is best.

Understanding vinegar

• Vinegar is made by adding the Acetobacter bacterium to a spirit, wine, or grain base. This causes the liquid to ferment and eventually oxidize, leading to the production of acetic acid.

• Chutneys, relishes, and similar preserves are quite forgiving in their requirements and can be made with any vinegar without having a detrimental effect on the finished product.

• Pickles are more exacting when it comes to the choice of vinegar. They require a vinegar with an acidity of at least 6 percent to ensure that they are preserved properly and hence keep well.

VINEGAR

• **Red and white wine vinegars** are usually 6 percent acid and are suitable for all pickle- and chutney-making. They have a good, clean flavor.

• **Cider vinegar** has an acidity of about 5 percent. It has a soft, smooth taste and is an excellent choice for chutneys and similar preserves, but it is not acidic enough for pickles.

• **Malt vinegars** usually have an acidity of 6 percent, making them suitable for all forms of chutneys and pickles. Natural malt vinegars have a distinct flavor; distilled malt vinegar is flavorless.

• **Rice wine vinegar** is a soft-tasting vinegar and tends to have an acidity of only 5 percent. Pickles made with it will not have a long shelf life and should be stored in the refrigerator.

SPICES

To ensure that they are at their most potent, dry spices should always be ground just before you need them. Few of us would relish a cup of coffee made from beans ground several months, let alone years, ago, but that is just what we often do when we need spices. Any flavoring that relies on volatile oils for its taste needs to be used as soon as possible after the oils have been released. I use a dedicated coffee grinder to grind spices, but a good result can be obtained using a mortar and pestle, plus a bit of hard work.

How to make chutneys and relishes

The excess water in fruits and vegetables must be driven off or it spoils the finished preserve. In chutneys and similar, this is achieved by long, slow boiling, which also gives a good mounding consistency. Sugar and vinegar are the preserving elements.

1 PREPARING THE INGREDIENTS

Chop the vegetables to an even size: ½in (1cm) cubes are about right. Larger dried fruits, such as dates and peaches, are also best chopped just before use. Finely grate ginger and garlic. Use a Microplane or similar grater to zest citrus fruit; when juicing the fruit, sieve to remove any seeds. Grind all whole spices using a coffee grinder or a mortar and pestle.

2 COOKING THE MIXTURE

Put all the ingredients in the preserving pot, and simmer over a low heat, stirring often to ensure that the sugar dissolves. Increase the heat to medium, and simmer the preserve until thick—this can take an hour or more. It is important to stir the mixture from time to time, especially toward the end of cooking, when it can stick to the bottom of the pan.

3 TESTING

To test whether the preserve is ready, drag a wooden spoon through the mixture on the bottom of the pan. The spoon should leave a clear path, with perhaps a little liquid seeping back. If the mixture flows back to cover the path, boil for a little longer.

4 REDUCING TO A PURÉE

For ketchups and sauces, there is an additional step, which involves reducing the cooked mixture to a purée. This is done by processing it in a blender, passing it through a food mill, or pushing it through a fine sieve.

COOKING THE MIXTURE

TESTING

COVERING WITH
VINEGAR

How to make pickles and vinegars

In pickles, salt is used to drive off the water in the vegetables that would otherwise dilute the vinegar used and hence spoil the final product. This is done either by brining or by dry-salting. Salt also seasons the pickles and contributes to the preserving process.

1 BRINING OR DRY-SALTING
Whether you brine or dry-salt the ingredients depends on the vegetables being used. Those with a high water content, such as cucumbers, cabbage, zucchini, and eggplants, are best dry-salted rather than brined.

Brining To make a typical brining solution, dissolve 8oz (225g) table salt in 6 cups water in a large glass, china, or plastic bowl. Immerse the prepared vegetables in the mixture and let stand for 12–24 hours. Drain, rinse well under cold running water, and spread out on clean dish towels to dry. Brine should always be used cold to avoid encouraging bacterial growth.

Dry-salting In a large glass, china, or plastic bowl, arrange the prepared vegetables in layers, sprinkling each layer with salt. Let stand overnight, then drain the vegetables, rinse under cold running water, and spread out on clean dish towels to dry.

2 COVERING WITH VINEGAR
Hot pickles are those that are cooked for only a short time, often as little as 2–3 minutes, while cold pickles generally have hot vinegar poured over the cold-packed vegetables. With hot pickles, the vegetables are brined, cooked for a short time to ensure the vegetables stay crisp, then potted in spiced vinegar. Cold pickles, on the other hand, are brined, then simply covered with spiced vinegar without prior cooking.

Summer berries

Blackberries • Black currants • Blueberries • Cranberries
Cherries • Gooseberries • Grapes • Loganberries
Raspberries • Strawberries

Picking berries from a late summer garden can yield a surprising number of varieties that provide the essential ingredients for pots of deliciously dark-hued jumbleberry jam—perfect for spreading on freshly made crusty bread.

Jumbleberry jam

⏱ TAKES 20 MINUTES   🍲 MAKES 1LB 10OZ (750G)   🥫 KEEPS FOR UP TO 1 YEAR

1 In a heavy, nonreactive pot, mix together the berries and sugar, then stir in the lemon juice. Warm the mixture over low heat, stirring gently, until the sugar dissolves.

2 Increase the heat and bring to a boil. Cook at a full rolling boil for 3–5 minutes until the jam reaches the setting point.

3 Ladle into hot sterilized jars, seal, and label.

INGREDIENTS

1lb (450g) mixed berries (raspberries, red currants, black currants, etc.)

1lb (450g) white granulated sugar

freshly squeezed juice of 1 large lemon

CHOOSING BERRIES

One of the great advantages of this recipe is that it doesn't matter precisely what proportions of different berries you use. It is the total weight that matters, and this must equal the weight of the sugar. If using strawberries, they will need to be hulled first, and currants will need to be destemmed.

Sue Laing, a good friend of mine who lives on a fruit farm in Norfolk, is justly famous for her jams. To achieve the right cooking heat, make separate batches rather than doubling quantities.

Sue's strawberry preserve

🕐 TAKES 25 MINUTES   🥘 MAKES 4LB (1.8KG)   🫙 KEEPS FOR 6–9 MONTHS

1 In a large china or glass bowl, layer the strawberries and sugar, then sprinkle with the juice. Cover with plastic wrap and let sit for 24 hours.

2 Scrape the contents of the bowl into a heavy, nonreactive pot and slowly bring to a boil. Let the mixture simmer over low heat for 5 minutes, then remove from the heat, cover, and let stand for 48 hours.

3 Return the pan to the heat, and bring the mixture back to a boil. Skim off any scum from the top. Boil until the mixture reaches the setting point. The jam will always be quite soft, so I boil it until it thickens to my liking.

4 Remove from the heat, ladle into hot sterilized jars, seal, and label.

INGREDIENTS

3lb 3oz (1.5kg) small, freshly picked strawberries

3lb 3oz (1.5kg) granulated sugar

freshly squeezed juice of 4 lemons

I like to make jam with cultivated blackberries and jelly with wild ones. The latter have masses of small seeds that I think are better removed, as they can be a bit intrusive in the finished preserve.

Blackberry jam

🕐 TAKES 15 MINUTES   🥘 MAKES 4LB (1.8KG)   🫙 KEEPS FOR UP TO 1 YEAR

1 Wash the berries, then drain them well, spreading them out on a paper towel to ensure as much water as possible is absorbed. Alternatively, let drain in a large sieve or colander.

2 Put in a large nonreactive pot with the lemon juice and sugar. Warm over low heat, stirring gently from time to time, until the sugar has dissolved and the berries have softened and released their juice.

3 Cook at a full rolling boil for 3 minutes. Stir in the pectin and boil for 2 minutes longer, then test for a set.

4 Once the jam has reached the setting point, ladle into hot sterilized jars, seal, and label.

INGREDIENTS

2¼lb (1kg) blackberries

freshly squeezed juice of 1 lemon

2¼lb (1kg) granulated sugar

4oz (125g) liquid pectin

This is a luxurious jam, perfect for an afternoon tea. It works well spread inside a sponge layer cake, too. I find it a useful jam to make with larger strawberries.

Strawberry, rhubarb, and vanilla jam

⏱ TAKES 20 MINUTES   🥄 MAKES 2¼LB (1.25KG)   🫙 KEEPS FOR UP TO 1 YEAR

1   Cut the rhubarb into 1in (2.5cm) lengths, then cut the strawberries into slices about ¼in (0.5cm) thick.

2   In a large china or glass bowl, layer the fruit with the sugar. Pour the lemon juice over the top and let sit in a cool place overnight.

3   Scrape the fruit, sugar, and all the juice into a heavy nonreactive pot, and warm over low heat. Stir from time to time, then bring the mixture to a full rolling boil. Cook for 2 minutes, then turn off the heat and stir in the pectin.

4   Return the mixture to a boil, and boil for 2 minutes longer or until the jam has reached the setting point. Remove from the heat, skim off any scum from the top of the jam, and stir in the vanilla seeds.

5   Let cool for 5 minutes before ladling into hot sterilized jars, sealing, and labeling.

VARIATION
For a spicier jam, replace the vanilla seeds with 2oz (60g) fresh ginger, peeled and finely grated.

INGREDIENTS

2¼lb (1.25kg) rhubarb

1lb 5oz (600g) strawberries

4lb (1.8kg) granulated sugar

freshly squeezed juice of 2 lemons

9oz (250g) liquid pectin

seeds scraped from 1 large vanilla bean

Preserving summer berries

CHOOSING FRUITS FOR A GOOD SET

Ripe, headily scented berries are what summer is all about. Pick-your-own farms, farm stands, and farmers' markets allow us access to quantities of beautifully ripe fruit, and this is what you need for making the best and most flavorful preserves. As the right balance of acid and pectin is necessary to obtain a set, slightly underripe berries or those just on the point of ripeness, which contain the highest levels of both, are the best choice. Pick your berries on a dry day.

High pectin

• **Black, white, and red currants** are high in both acid and pectin. They can be combined with other fruit to help facilitate a set. Make sure you remove all the stems.
• **Gooseberries** can be used fully ripe, as they are high in both acid and pectin. The juice can be used to add pectin to soft-setting jams such as strawberry. Some varieties of green gooseberry produce pink jam.
• **Cranberries** usually contain sufficient pectin to make both jams and jellies, without the need for extra to be added. Look for dry and unshriveled bright red berries, and store in the refrigerator until needed.

Moderate pectin

• **Raspberries** have moderate amounts of acid and pectin, and are highly scented and flavored. Choose uncrushed whole, ripe berries. Use soon after harvest, as they are fragile and ferment easily.
• **Loganberries, tayberries, and boysenberries** are a cross between blackberries and raspberries. They contain moderate amounts of acid and pectin. Used with raspberries, they will give both a deeper color and more pronounced flavor.

CURRANTS of all colors are pectin- and acid-rich.

RASPBERRIES are among the most popular berries for preserving and need some added pectin to aid setting.

Low pectin

- **Strawberries** are low in both acid and pectin. Look for small, firm, slightly underripe berries.
- **Blueberries** contain little acid or pectin, and are best used for preserves when fully ripe.
- **Blackberries**, if cultivated, contain more acid than their wild cousins. Avoid berries that are dusty. Late-season berries contain less acid and pectin, so add apples for a good set.

BLUEBERRIES AND STRAWBERRIES require added pectin for a set.

Loganberries are a hybrid made by crossing raspberries with blackberries. Their flavor is more tart than raspberries and, like blackberries, tend to retain a white inner core. This makes them more time-consuming to prepare, as the cores must be removed before cooking.

Loganberry jam

⏱ TAKES 20 MINUTES　　🍲 MAKES 3LB (1.35KG)　　🥫 KEEPS FOR UP TO 1 YEAR

1　Remove the white cores from the berries. Put the berries and sugar in a heavy nonreactive pot and cook over low heat until the sugar dissolves and the fruit softens.

2　Bring to a boil and boil rapidly for 5 to 7 minutes, or until the jam has just reached the setting point.

3　Ladle into hot sterilized jars, seal, and label. If you prefer a seedless jam, sieve before ladling.

INGREDIENTS

1lb 10oz (750g) loganberries

1lb 10oz (750g) granulated sugar

Gooseberries have both a high acid and a high pectin content, so this tart jam sets quickly and is one of the easiest to make. The color will vary, depending on the variety and ripeness of the berries. The tartness of this delicious jam makes it a perfect foil for scones and cream.

Gooseberry jam

⏱ TAKES 10 MINUTES　　🍲 MAKES 4½LB (2KG)　　🥫 KEEPS FOR UP TO 1 YEAR

1　Remove the tops and tails from the gooseberries (this takes some time, but improves the finished jam). Wash the berries, shake off any excess water, and put in a large nonreactive pot with ½ cup water.

2　Cover and bring to a boil. Reduce the heat, and simmer for about 5 minutes until the berries are very soft.

3　Remove the lid and stir in the sugar. When the sugar has dissolved, increase the heat and boil rapidly for about 2 minutes until the jam has reached the setting point.

4　Ladle into hot sterilized jars, seal, and label.

INGREDIENTS

2¼lb (1kg) gooseberries

2¾lb (1.25kg) granulated sugar

It's important to cook currants well before adding the sugar or they will become as tough as tiny bullets. Once this has been done, and the sugar added, reaching the setting point will not take long. Black currants should be as fresh as possible—the older they are, the tougher the skins.

Black currant jam

🕐 TAKES 30–40 MINUTES   🍲 MAKES 4½LB (2KG)   🫙 KEEPS FOR UP TO 1 YEAR

1   Wash the currants well to remove any dust and grit. Drain and put in a heavy nonreactive pot with 3½ cups water.

2   Bring to a boil, cover, and simmer the mixture over low heat for about 20 minutes until the fruit is very soft.

3   Add the sugar, stirring gently until dissolved. Increase the heat and boil rapidly for about 15 minutes until the jam reaches the setting point.

4   Ladle into hot sterilized jars, seal, and label.

INGREDIENTS

2¼lb (1kg) black currants

3lb (1.35kg) granulated sugar

Cranberries are often overlooked as a breakfast preserve, being more often considered an accompaniment to roast turkey. This tangy jam redresses the balance, and has a good color and flavor. Enjoy it with hot buttered toast, biscuits, or English muffins.

Cranberry and orange preserve

🕐 TAKES 25 MINUTES   🍲 MAKES 1LB 7OZ (650G)   🫙 KEEPS FOR UP TO 1 YEAR

1   Put the cranberries and orange juice in a large nonreactive pot, cover, and cook over medium heat for about 15 minutes until the fruit is very soft.

2   Stir in the sugar and zest, and cook over low heat until the sugar has dissolved. Increase the heat and cook at a full rolling boil for 3–5 minutes until the preserve reaches the setting point.

3   Ladle into hot sterilized jars, seal, and label.

INGREDIENTS

1lb 2oz (500g) fresh cranberries

freshly squeezed juice of 3 oranges

1lb 2oz (500g) granulated sugar

grated zest of 2 oranges

This is probably my favorite recipe for jam. It reminds me of summer days, the heady scent of fruit at the pick-your-own farm, and traditional English teas of jam, scones, and cream in the garden. I always make small batches, as this jam is best eaten fresh. Don't look for a firm set—the best raspberry jam should always be a little runny.

Best-ever raspberry jam

TAKES 15–20 MINUTES   MAKES 2LB (900G)   KEEPS FOR UP TO 1 YEAR

1 Put the berries and sugar in a heavy nonreactive pot. Simmer over low heat, stirring occasionally, until the fruit has softened and the sugar has dissolved.

2 Bring to a boil and boil rapidly for 5–7 minutes until the mixture reaches the setting point.

3 Ladle into hot sterilized jars, seal, and label.

INGREDIENTS

1lb (450g) freshly picked raspberries

1lb (450g) granulated sugar

VARIATION
In winter, when snow is abundant, evoke the scent of summer by making this jam with frozen raspberries instead of fresh ones.

RETAINING THE SEEDS

Some folks worry about the seeds in this jam. If you are one of them, by all means sieve out the seeds while the jam is hot. Be forewarned, though, that in doing so you will reduce the weight—and also, I believe, the flavor—of the jam. After all, you would not discard the seeds from fresh raspberries …

Lemon curd is a well-known, perennial favorite, but curds can be made with a wide variety of fruit. I love raspberry curd. Use it to fill roulades and sponge cakes, or fold it into lightly whipped cream and pipe into meringues for an irresistible treat.

Raspberry curd

⏱ TAKES 30–40 MINUTES   🥘 MAKES 3½LB (1.6KG)   🥫 KEEPS FOR ABOUT 3 MONTHS

1   Put the berries and 2 tablespoons of water in a large saucepan, and bring to a boil. Simmer, covered, for 5 minutes or until the fruit is very soft.

2   To remove the seeds, press the mixture through a sieve into the top half of a large double boiler. If you don't have one, you can cook this curd in a heatproof bowl over a pan of simmering water.

3   Add the sugar, butter, and eggs. Place over the lowest possible heat and, using a balloon whisk, gently whisk the mixture until the sugar has dissolved and the butter has melted.

4   Continue to simmer, stirring constantly with a wooden spoon, until the mixture thickens, then turn off the heat and stir again. If the curd isn't quite thick enough, heat again, but remember that it will thicken further as it cools.

5   When the curd has reached the desired consistency, ladle into hot sterilized jars, and label. Store in the refrigerator.

INGREDIENTS

2¼lb (1kg) raspberries

1lb (450g) granulated sugar

1 stick (4oz or 115g) salted butter, diced

4 large eggs, beaten

EXTRA EQUIPMENT

double boiler (optional)

PREVENTING CURDLING

Stir with a wooden spoon and keep the mixture moving while you cook to ensure it does not stick to the pan. On no account must it boil or it may curdle. At the first sign of bubbles, remove from the heat immediately, set the top half of the pan (or heatproof bowl) in a large bowl of ice water, and stir the curd with the wooden spoon. The curd has reached the right consistency when it coats the back of the spoon.

Although this preserve does require you to pit the cherries—which can be a messy job—its wonderful taste and scent make it worth the extra bother. To ease the task, invite a friend to keep you company while you work. Making this jam is a wonderful way to use up an excess of cherries from a heavy summer crop.

Black cherry preserve

🕐 TAKES 30 MINUTES   🍲 MAKES 3LB (1.35KG)   🫙 KEEPS FOR UP TO 1 YEAR

1 If using fresh cherries, remove any stems and pits, using rubber gloves to protect your hands from staining.

2 Put the cherries and ⅔ cup water in a large nonreactive pot, and bring to a boil. Cover and simmer for about 15 minutes until the cherries are tender. Turn off the heat and add the sugar and lemon juice, stirring until the sugar dissolves.

3 Return the mixture to a boil, and boil for 2 minutes, stirring occasionally and skimming off any scum that rises to the surface. Turn off the heat again, add the pectin, and stir in well.

4 Cook at a full rolling boil for another 8–10 minutes, then test for a set. Once the jam has reached the setting point, ladle into hot sterilized jars, seal, and label.

VARIATION

For those who do not have the time—or the inclination—to pit the fruit, frozen cherries come already pitted and work well in this recipe.

INGREDIENTS

2¼lb (1kg) cherries

2¼lb (1kg) granulated sugar

freshly squeezed juice of 2 lemons

9oz (250g) liquid pectin

I have a small Morello cherry tree in my garden, so I make a few pots of this delicious jam each year. Morello cherries are wonderfully colored but quite small, which means that pitting them is a labor of love. Enhance plain yogurt with a generous swirl of this jam, or use it as a topping for hot buttered biscuits or scones on crisp winter Sundays.

Morello cherry jam

🕐 TAKES 10 MINUTES   🍲 MAKES 3LB (1.35KG)   🫙 KEEPS FOR UP TO 1 YEAR

1 Begin by pitting the cherries, using rubber gloves to protect your hands from staining.

2 Put the cherries, sugar, and lemon juice in a heavy nonreactive pot, and simmer over low heat, stirring to dissolve the sugar. Bring the mixture to a boil, then reduce the heat and simmer for 5 minutes or until the cherries are cooked.

3 Stir in the pectin. Boil for 2 minutes before turning off the heat and testing for a set.

4 When the jam has reached the setting point, ladle into hot sterilized jars, seal, and label.

VARIATION
For an altogether more decadent preserve, add ⅓ cup kirsch to the jam once the setting point has been reached, and stir in well. The jam will be a little softer, but delicious.

INGREDIENTS

2¼lb (1kg) Morello cherries

1lb 10oz (750g) granulated sugar

freshly squeezed juice of 2 lemons

4½oz (125g) liquid pectin

To prevent them from becoming tough and chewy, blueberries should always be well cooked before the sugar is added. As they are low in acid and pectin, you need to add both of these ingredients for a successful preserve. Blueberry jam goes well with pancakes, or it may be swirled into plain yogurt or used as a filling for a layer cake.

Blueberry preserve

🕐 TAKES 30 MINUTES   🍲 MAKES 3LB (1.6KG)   🫙 KEEPS FOR UP TO 1 YEAR

1   Put the blueberries in a heavy nonreactive pot with ⅔ cup water and the lemon juice. Bring the mixture to a boil, then reduce the heat, cover, and simmer for 10 minutes or until the fruit is soft.

2   Add the sugar, stirring over low heat until the sugar has dissolved. Increase the heat and boil rapidly for 3–4 minutes.

3   Add the pectin and boil for another minute before turning off the heat and testing for a set.

4   When the jam has reached the setting point, ladle into hot sterilized jars, seal, and label.

VARIATION
Wild blueberries work well in this recipe. Being smaller than cultivated blueberries does not mean wild ones need less cooking time, though— they must be boiled until soft before you add the sugar.

INGREDIENTS

2¼lb (1kg) blueberries

freshly squeezed juice of 4 lemons

2¼lb (1kg) granulated sugar

½ cup liquid pectin

Traditionally used in peanut butter and jelly sandwiches, grape jelly is best made with very fresh, slightly underripe grapes—perfect if you have a prolific vine in your yard.

Grape jelly

🕐 TAKES 25 MINUTES   🍲 MAKES 1¾LB (800G)   🫙 KEEPS FOR UP TO 1 YEAR

1   Put the grapes—which can be a mixture of red and white—in a stainless-steel saucepan and crush them: I use a potato masher. Add ⅔ cup water, then bring to a boil, reduce the heat, cover, and simmer for 10–15 minutes until the grapes are very soft.

2   Crush the grapes again, then spoon the mixture into a cheesecloth or other jelly bag and allow to drip for 12 hours.

3   Measure the juice, then measure out the correct amount of sugar, pectin, and lemon juice. Put the juice and sugar in a heavy nonreactive pot, and bring slowly to a boil, stirring until the sugar has dissolved.

4   Add the pectin, increase the heat, and boil rapidly for 3–5 minutes until the jelly has set. Ladle into hot sterilized jars, seal, and label.

INGREDIENTS

2¼lb (1kg) grapes

FOR EVERY 2 CUPS JUICE

1½lb (675g) superfine sugar

3½oz (100g) liquid pectin

freshly squeezed juice of 1 large lemon

Use a relatively inexpensive port and either well-scrubbed or unwaxed fruit for this good all-around jelly. For a more savory version, stir in 1 tablespoon chopped rosemary with the zests.

Port wine and orange jelly

🕐 TAKES 15 MINUTES   🍲 MAKES 3½LB (1.6KG)   🫙 KEEPS FOR UP TO 1 YEAR

1   Put the port, orange and lemon juice, and sugar in a large nonreactive pot, and bring the mixture slowly to a boil.

2   Once the sugar has dissolved, bring to a full rolling boil and cook for 10–15 minutes. Add the pectin and boil for another 2 minutes, skimming off any scum from the top of the jelly.

3   Turn off the heat and test for a set. If the jelly has reached the setting point, stir in the orange and lemon zest. Boil for 30 seconds.

4   Turn off the heat and let the jelly stand for 3–4 minutes to cool slightly, then ladle into hot sterilized jars, seal, and label.

INGREDIENTS

3 cups red port

grated zest and juice of 3 large oranges

grated zest and juice of 1 lemon

2¼lb (1kg) granulated sugar

9oz (250g) liquid pectin

This recipe makes a delicious clear preserve. Made with Shiraz wine, the result will be a beautiful amber-colored jelly to partner with scones or cold meats.

Shiraz wine jelly

🕐 TAKES 20 MINUTES   🍲 MAKES 2¼LB (1KG)   🫙 KEEPS FOR UP TO 1 YEAR

1   In a heavy nonreactive pot, mix the wine with the lemon juice and pectin. Bring to a boil, whisking from time to time to ensure that all the ingredients are thoroughly combined.

2   Add the sugar and stir the mixture over low heat until the sugar has dissolved completely.

3   Increase the heat and bring the mixture to a full rolling boil, using a slotted spoon to skim off any scum that rises to the surface during cooking. Boil for 2 minutes, then turn off the heat and test for a set.

4   If the jelly has not set, return the mixture to a boil and cook at a full rolling boil for another minute, then test again for a set.

5   When the jelly has reached the setting point, ladle into small hot sterilized jars, seal, and label.

VARIATION
Any full-bodied wine can be used to make this preserve. Try Chardonnay or port instead of Shiraz.

INGREDIENTS

3 cups Shiraz wine

freshly squeezed juice of 2 large lemons

9oz (250g) liquid pectin

2lb (900g) granulated sugar

The astringent flavor and bright red skins of cranberries add both acid and color to jams, jellies, relishes, and ketchups. This jelly is the classic accompaniment to those Thanksgiving and Christmas turkey dinners. Easy to make and pretty to look at, it is the perfect seasonal gift.

Cranberry jelly

TAKES 45 MINUTES   MAKES 1¾LB (800G)   KEEPS FOR UP TO 1 YEAR

1　Put the berries and 4 cups water in a nonreactive saucepan and bring to a boil, then reduce the heat and simmer, covered, for 25–30 minutes until the fruit is very soft.

2　Mash the mixture well—a potato masher does a good job—then spoon into a cheesecloth or other jelly bag and let drip overnight.

3　Measure the resulting liquid: you should have about 3 cups. If you have more, boil rapidly to reduce to this quantity; if less, add water to make up to the correct quantity.

4　Pour the liquid into a nonreactive pot and add the sugar. Cook over low heat until the sugar dissolves, then increase the heat and cook at a full rolling boil for about 15 minutes. Test for a set.

5　Once the jelly has reached the setting point, skim off any scum from the top, then pot the jelly into hot sterilized jars, seal, and label.

VARIATION
The grated zest and juice of 2 oranges can be added to the fruit before cooking—or try a 4in (10cm) cinnamon stick, lightly crushed.

INGREDIENTS

1lb (450g) cranberries

1lb 2oz (500g) granulated sugar

This scrumptious jelly has all the flavor of raspberry jam, but none of the seeds. Simple to produce, and easily made with frozen berries, it needs neither acid nor pectin.

Raspberry jelly

⏱ TAKES 20 MINUTES 🍲 MAKES 2¼LB (1KG) 🫙 KEEPS FOR UP TO 1 YEAR

1 Put the berries and 1¼ cups water in a nonreactive saucepan and bring to a boil. Reduce the heat and simmer for 10–15 minutes until the berries are soft. Spoon into a cheesecloth or other jelly bag and allow to drip overnight.

2 Measure the juice, then measure the sugar in the correct proportion. For 3 cups juice, you will need 1lb 10oz (750g) sugar. Pour the juice into a clean nonreactive pot and stir in the sugar.

3 Warm the mixture over low heat until the sugar has dissolved, then increase the heat and boil rapidly for about 5 minutes. Skim off any scum from the jelly as it rises to the surface.

4 Turn off the heat and test for a set. When the jam has reached the setting point, ladle into hot sterilized jars, seal, and label.

INGREDIENTS

2¼lb (1kg) raspberries, thawed if frozen

3½oz (100g) granulated sugar for every 3½fl oz (100ml) juice

High in pectin and acid, and needing only sugar for a good set, red currants make a delightful preserve for both sweet and savory dishes. Try black currants or white currants, too.

Red currant jelly

⏱ TAKES 40 MINUTES 🍲 MAKES 800G (1¾LB) 🫙 KEEPS FOR UP TO 1 YEAR

1 Put the fruit and 2 cups water in a heavy nonreactive pot. Bring to a boil, cover, and simmer for 30 minutes or until the fruit is soft.

2 Mash lightly—a potato masher is ideal for this—then spoon into a jelly bag and allow the mixture to drip for 12 hours or overnight.

3 Measure the resulting juice and the appropriate quantity of sugar. Put both in a clean nonreactive pot. Stir over low heat until the sugar has dissolved, then boil rapidly until the setting point has been reached.

4 Ladle into hot sterilized jars, seal, and label.

INGREDIENTS

2¼lb (1kg) red currants

1lb 2oz (500g) granulated sugar for every 2 cups juice

Fruit vinegars not only taste good, but are also wonderfully colored and make a refreshing change from balsamic. Slightly sweet, they go well with goat cheese salads and fish dishes.

Berry vinegar

🕐 TAKES 5 MINUTES 🍲 MAKES 2 CUPS 🥫 KEEPS FOR 3–6 MONTHS

1 Put the berries and sugar in a nonreactive saucepan and heat gently, stirring occasionally, until the berries are soft and release their juices and the sugar has dissolved.

2 Transfer the mixture to a glass jar or bowl, and stir in the vinegar. Cover with plastic wrap and let sit to infuse for at least 1 week, but preferably 3 weeks.

3 Strain the vinegar into a clean bottle and use for dressings.

INGREDIENTS

9oz (250g) blackberries, raspberries or black currants, thawed if frozen

2oz (60g) superfine sugar

14fl oz (400ml) white wine vinegar

I make this lovely drink each December to serve, ice cold, in tiny liqueur glasses after dinner. The color is wonderfully festive and the cranberries are rich in vitamin C, making this almost a drink that is good for you! Don't forget to save the original vodka bottle and its screwtop lid, as you will need them for storing the drink after the initial infusing.

Frozen cranberry vodka

🕐 TAKES 5 MINUTES 🍲 MAKES 3 CUPS 🥫 KEEPS FOR 1 YEAR, FROZEN

1 Put the cranberries and sugar in a food processor or blender and process, pulsing the machine on and off, until the berries are finely chopped.

2 Transfer the mixture to a glass or china bowl, and pour in the vodka. Stir and cover with a double layer of plastic wrap. Leave the bowl in a cool, dark place for 3–4 weeks.

3 Strain the mixture through cheesecloth or muslin and pour back into the saved vodka bottle. Screw on the lid and store in the freezer until needed.

INGREDIENTS

1lb (450g) cranberries

8oz (225g) granulated sugar

3 cups (750ml) vodka

Homemade drinks that mimic French cordials are simple to put together. I make this fruity gin as well as cassis, raspberry vodka, and both blackberry and cranberry vodka (see p47). Use generic-brand spirits and really fresh, ripe fruit. Pour the drinks back into the original bottles and, when ready, serve either as liqueurs or diluted with a splash of white wine.

Raspberry gin

🕐 TAKES 15 MINUTES   🍲 MAKES 3 CUPS   🥫 KEEPS FOR 1–2 YEARS

1 Put the raspberries and sugar in a nonreactive saucepan and heat gently, stirring occasionally, until the berries are soft and release their juices and the sugar has dissolved.

2 Transfer the mixture to a glass bowl or jar, and pour in the gin. Stir, then cover with plastic wrap, sealing tightly.

3 Stir daily for 4 to 5 days, then strain into a clean bottle, seal, and store in a cupboard or dark pantry, or in the freezer. Taste after about 8 weeks, adding more sugar if you think it is necessary. The gin is ready to drink after about 3 months, but is best left for 1 year. Add a few fresh raspberries to each glass when serving, if desired.

VARIATION
For blackberry vodka, replace the raspberries with blackberries and the gin with vodka. Store in the freezer after making.

INGREDIENTS

1lb (450g) raspberries, plus extra for serving (optional)

8oz (225g) granulated sugar

1 pint (600ml) gin

Stone fruits

Apricots • Damsons • Greengages • Mirabelles
Nectarines • Peaches
Plums • Prunes

This is a wonderfully fragrant jam, vying with raspberry as my very favorite—perfect on hot buttered toast, spooned onto scones, or as a luscious and slightly tart filling for sponge cakes. Be sure to use apricots that are fully ripe but still firm.

Apricot jam

⏱ TAKES 25 MINUTES   🍲 MAKES 2¾LB (1.25KG)   🥫 KEEPS FOR 9 MONTHS

1   Cut the apricots into quarters and remove the pits. Put the fruit, 1¾ cups water, and lemon juice in a heavy nonreactive pot, and bring the mixture to a boil. Simmer over low heat, stirring occasionally, for about 15 minutes until the fruit is very soft.

2   Add the sugar, allowing it to dissolve into the fruit. Try not to stir the mixture too much, as this will break up the apricots—you want to retain some large chunks to give the jam texture.

3   Increase the heat and bring the mixture to a full rolling boil. Boil for 4–5 minutes, then stir in the pectin and boil for another 2 minutes. If making the jam without pectin, it will need to be cooked at a full rolling boil for 15 minutes: this will produce a softer jam.

4   Remove from the heat and test for a set.

5   When the jam has reached the setting point, ladle it into hot sterilized jars, seal, and label.

INGREDIENTS

2¼lb (1kg) just-ripe apricots

freshly squeezed juice of 3 lemons

2¼lb (1kg) granulated sugar

4½oz (125g) liquid pectin (optional)

CHOOSING FRUIT

I prefer to look for larger apricots when making this preserve, as I find them better for jam than smaller, sweeter ones. To make the most of the finished jam, choose fruit that is fragrant, just-ripe, and blemish-free.

This jam is very simple to make because you do not need to test for a set. Based on dried apricots, all it requires is simmering until thick. Lime juice and zest add the necessary tartness. Make this preserve to bring cheer to dark winter days when fresh fruit is hard to come by.

Apricot and lime jam

🕐 TAKES 30 MINUTES   🍲 MAKES 1LB 2OZ (500G)   🫙 KEEPS FOR 1 YEAR

1   Ready-to-eat dried apricots require no pre-soaking, so you can use them straight from the package. Chop the apricots coarsely, then transfer to a heavy nonreactive pot. Add 2⅓ cups water and the lime zest and juice. Bring to a boil, reduce the heat, and simmer the mixture for 10–15 minutes until the apricots are tender.

2   Now add the sugar, stirring over low heat until it has dissolved.

3   Increase the heat to medium, and continue to simmer for about 15 minutes depending on the size of the pan, stirring occasionally, until the jam is thick.

4   Ladle into hot sterilized jars, seal, and label.

VARIATION
Dried peaches or dried pears could replace the apricots in this recipe. If using dried pears, I like to chop in some sugared crystallized ginger, too, for extra zing.

INGREDIENTS

8oz (225g) dried apricots

finely grated zest and freshly squeezed juice of 1 lime

8oz (225g) granulated sugar

Fruit cheeses are really concentrated fruit purées, spiced and cooked until firm enough to slice. They are delicious with both meat and cheese. This recipe is ideal for damsons, as it allows the small fruits to be cooked whole, then rubbed through a sieve to remove skins and pits.

Damson cheese

⏱ TAKES 90 MINUTES   🍲 MAKES 2¼LB (1KG)   🥫 KEEPS FOR 1 YEAR

1 Put the damsons and 4 cups water in a large nonreactive pot. Using a mallet or rolling pin, crush the ginger coarsely, then add to the pot. Bring the mixture to a boil, then reduce the heat and simmer for 30 minutes or until the fruit is very soft.

2 Let the fruit cool a little, then press through a sieve to remove the pits, skins, and remains of the ginger.

3 Pour the resulting purée into the cleaned nonreactive pot, and add the sugar. Place the pan over low heat, and stir frequently until the sugar has dissolved.

4 Increase the heat to medium and let the mixture cook for 30–45 minutes until reduced and very thick. You will need to watch carefully toward the end of cooking, as the fruit can stick and burn.

5 To test if the cheese is cooked, scoop out a spoonful, put it on a cold plate, and let it cool. It should stay in a mound rather than spread out over the plate. Always remember to turn the heat off from under the pot of jam or cheese while you test for a set.

6 When the cheese has reached the setting point, ladle into hot sterilized jars, seal, and label.

INGREDIENTS

4½lb (2kg) damson plums

4in (10cm) piece of fresh root ginger

3lb 3oz (1.5kg) granulated sugar

Plums are packed full of pectin, so jams made with them set easily. Choosing a variety isn't a problem for this recipe, but larger plums are easier to prepare. Cinnamon is a spice that works especially well with plums. For a stylish touch, add a piece of cinnamon stick to each jar.

Red plum and cinnamon jam

🕐 TAKES 20 MINUTES   🍲 MAKES 2¾LB (1.25KG)   🥫 KEEPS FOR UP TO 1 YEAR

1 Cut the plums into halves or quarters, depending on size. Remove the pits and discard them.

2 Put the prepared fruit in a nonreactive pot, and add 1 cup water, the sugar, and the cinnamon. Cook gently over medium heat for 10–15 minutes, stirring, until the sugar has dissolved.

3 Increase the heat, bring to a full rolling boil, and cook for 3–5 minutes until the jam has reached the setting point.

4 Ladle into hot sterilized jars, adding a cinnamon stick to each one, if desired. Seal and label.

INGREDIENTS

2¼lb (1kg) red plums

2¼lb (1kg) granulated sugar

4in (10cm) cinnamon stick, finely ground in a spice mill, plus extra sticks for the jars (optional)

WATCHING FOR A SET

As plums contain a high quantity of pectin, watch carefully for a set—cook for a few minutes too long and the jam will be very thick and stiff. This jam is made with red plums, which is my family's preference, but yellow plum jam tastes good, too.

Preserving with plums

VARIETY OF USES

There are literally thousands of varieties of plums, and every one has its place in the making of preserves, jams, or chutneys. Plums can be the base for fruit sauces and ketchups, can add bulk to chutneys, and were often the base fruit of "red jam." High in pectin and acid, they set easily and so are a dream fruit for novice jam-makers.

What to look for

For jams and preserves, choose firm, just-ripe plums with a bloom on the skin and no blemishes. For sauces, ketchups, and jellies, you can use overripe or slightly less perfect plums, as long as you cut away all the bruises. Always avoid any fruit with mold, as this will taint the preserve. Plum jam tends to be quite plain in flavor, so try adding spices to enhance the taste. Cinnamon works well, as do vanilla, five-spice powder, and star anise.

GREENGAGE

PREPARATION AND USES

Plums may be divided into three main categories:
Small plums, such as damsons, mirabelles, and sloes, are better suited to jelly-making because pitting them is time-consuming.
Larger plums, such as Victoria, Santa Rosa, and President, are best cut into quarters before cooking.
Greengages are in a category of their own. They make the most delicious of plum jams and need no additional spicing.

FORTUNE RED

MIRABELLES

DAMSONS

PRESIDENT

GOLDEN PLUM

SANTA ROSA

In France, greengages are known by the wonderful name Reine Claude. *They are smaller than many plums, but make a scrumptious preserve. I like to use slightly less sugar than usual with this fruit to preserve as much of the fresh taste as possible. While the skin and flesh of the ripe fruit are a delightful yellowish-green, cooking can change the color of the finished jam.*

Greengage jam

🕐 TAKES 15–20 MINUTES   🍲 MAKES 2¼LB (1KG)   🥫 KEEPS FOR 6 MONTHS

1 Cut the greengages into quarters, removing and discarding all the pits.

2 Put the fruit and 7fl oz (200ml) water in a heavy nonreactive pot. Place over low heat and gently cook the mixture for 10 minutes, stirring from time to time, until the greengages soften and release their juices.

3 Add the sugar and continue to simmer, stirring, until all the sugar has dissolved.

4 Increase the heat, bring the mixture to a full rolling boil, and cook rapidly for about 5 minutes, skimming off any scum that rises to the surface. Test for a set.

5 Once the jam has reached the setting point, ladle into hot sterilized jars, seal, and label.

INGREDIENTS

2¼lb (1kg) greengage plums

1lb 10oz (750g) granulated sugar

Nuts add an interesting texture to this delightful summer preserve. I store all my nuts in the freezer to ensure that they stay as fresh as possible. Let them thaw completely before chopping them. Ladled into pretty jars and tied with ribbons, this preserve makes a lovely gift.

Peach and pistachio preserve

🕐 TAKES 20 MINUTES　　🍲 MAKES 2¾LB (1.25KG)　　🪣 KEEPS FOR 6–9 MONTHS

1　First, peel the peaches. Bring a large saucepan of water to a boil. Meanwhile, cut a cross in the base of each peach. When the water is boiling, drop in the fruit, turn off the heat, and leave for 3–4 minutes. Lift one peach from the water and see if the skin slips off easily. If it does, drain the remaining peaches. If not, return the peach to the water and wait for another 2–3 minutes before draining all the fruit and peeling it.

2　Chop the peach flesh into ½in (1cm) dice, discarding the pits.

3　Put the peach flesh, sugar, and lemon juice in a heavy nonreactive pot, and bring the mixture slowly to a boil. Cook at a full rolling boil for 4–5 minutes, skimming off any scum that rises to the surface.

4　Stir in the chopped nuts and the pectin, and simmer for 1 minute before testing for a set.

5　Once the preserve has reached the setting point, ladle into hot sterilized jars, seal, and label.

INGREDIENTS

2¼lb (1kg) ripe peaches

1¾lb (800g) granulated sugar

freshly squeezed juice of 2 lemons

2oz (60g) shelled pistachio nuts, chopped

4½oz (125g) liquid pectin

"Sugaring" the nectarines overnight draws out the juice, which dissolves the sugar. This sugary liquid is then boiled down first, so that the fruit is cooked for less time and remains chunky.

Nectarine conserve

🕐 TAKES 15 MINUTES   MAKES 3½LB (1.6KG)   KEEPS FOR 6–9 MONTHS

1 Cut the nectarines into ½in (1cm) cubes. In a large, clean glass or china bowl, arrange the nectarines in alternate layers with the sugar, continuing until all the fruit and sugar have been used. Pour in the lemon juice, cover with a towel or cloth, and let sit overnight.

2 Carefully lift the fruit from the liquid using a slotted spoon, or drain in a sieve set over a bowl. Reserve the liquid and set the fruit aside.

3 Scrape all the liquid and any undissolved sugar into a nonreactive pot. Heat slowly, stirring, until the sugar has dissolved. Boil rapidly for 5 minutes, then add the fruit and cook for another 5 minutes.

4 Add the pectin and cook at a full rolling boil for 2 minutes or until the setting point is reached. Ladle into hot sterilized jars, seal, and label.

INGREDIENTS

2¼lb (1kg) ripe nectarines

2¼lb (1kg) granulated sugar

freshly squeezed juice of 2 lemons

4½oz (125g) liquid pectin

There is no need to skin the peaches for this lovely pink jelly. Red currants replace added pectin and acid, making for a freshly flavored preserve.

Peach and red currant jelly

🕐 TAKES 25 MINUTES   MAKES 3LB 3OZ (1.5KG)   KEEPS FOR 6–9 MONTHS

1 Cut the peaches into 1½in (1cm) dice, discarding the pits. Put in a large nonreactive pot with the currants and 2 cups water. Bring to a boil, then simmer for about 20 minutes until very soft.

2 Spoon the mixture into a cheesecloth or other jelly bag positioned over a clean bowl and allow to drip overnight. Put the juice in the cleaned nonreactive pot; you should have about 3 cups. Add the sugar. Stir over low heat until the sugar has dissolved.

3 Increase the heat and cook at a full rolling boil for 3–5 minutes until the setting point is reached. Ladle into hot sterilized jars, seal, and label.

INGREDIENTS

2¼lb (1kg) ripe peaches

14oz (400g) red currants, stems removed

1lb 10oz (750g) granulated sugar

Tiny yellow plums with a distinctive flavor, mirabelles are more suited to jelly-making than to jams, as pitting them is time-consuming work. This preserve has a lovely color and sets well.

Mirabelle jelly

⏱ TAKES 30 MINUTES 🍲 MAKES 2¾LB (1.25KG) 🥫 KEEPS FOR 6–9 MONTHS

1   Put the mirabelles and 2 cups water in a saucepan, and simmer for 15–20 minutes until the fruit is very soft.

2   Spoon the mixture into a jelly bag, and let drip overnight.

3   Measure the resulting juice: you will have about 2⅓ cups. Weigh out the correct amount of sugar. Pour the mirabelle juice into a heavy nonreactive pot, and add the lemon juice and sugar.

4   Bring the mixture slowly to a boil, then simmer for 2–3 minutes, stirring frequently, until the sugar dissolves. Cook at a full rolling boil for 2–3 minutes, skimming off any scum. Test for a set.

5   Once the jelly has reached the setting point, ladle into hot sterilized jars, seal, and label.

INGREDIENTS

2¼lb (1kg) mirabelle plums

3oz (90g) granulated sugar for every 3½fl oz (100ml) mirabelle juice

freshly squeezed juice of 2 lemons

These prunes are wonderful spooned over ice cream, eaten for a special breakfast with Greek-style yogurt, or baked in rich almond cakes.

Prunes in brandy

⏱ TAKES 25 MINUTES 🍲 MAKES 1LB 2OZ (500G) 🥫 KEEPS FOR 2 YEARS

1   Make 4 quarts of tea from the tea leaves. Strain the brewed tea into a bowl and add the prunes, making sure they are completely covered. Let soak overnight.

2   Drain the prunes well, patting them dry with paper towels.

3   Pack the prunes into 2 x 9oz (250g) jars, adding 2–3 tablespoons sugar to each jar and pouring in enough brandy to cover the fruit.

4   Seal, label, and store. The prunes will be ready to eat in 3–4 months. Both the prunes and the brandy can be consumed.

INGREDIENTS

1 tsp Earl Grey or other tea leaves

1lb 2oz (500g) prunes

4–6 tbsp raw or light brown or muscovado sugar, per jar

14fl oz (400ml) brandy, plus extra to cover if needed, per jar

This dual-purpose recipe comes from my summer holidays in central France. The peaches make a heady topping for ice cream and the brandy on its own is a delicious sticky after-dinner liqueur. For a simple but enticing dessert, whisk some of the flavored brandy into whipped cream, add the chopped fruit and some crumbled meringue, then spoon into wine goblets.

Peaches in brandy

🕐 NO COOKING   🍲 MAKES ONE ½-GALLON (2-LITER) JAR   🍶 KEEPS FOR 6–9 MONTHS

1   Cut a small cross in the base of each peach, then put them in a deep bowl. Cover the fruit with boiling water and let sit for 2 minutes. Remove a peach from the water and try to peel the skin. If the skin comes away easily, drain and peel all of the fruit. If not, leave in the water for another minute.

2   Cut the peaches into quarters and discard the pits. Arrange in layers in the jar, alternating with layers of sugar. Push the vanilla bean down one side of the jar.

3   Pour in the brandy, then seal and label the jar, shaking it gently to help the sugar dissolve.

4   Leave the jar in a cool, dark place for about 3 months, shaking gently about once a week. I serve the brandy straight from the jar, but you can strain it into a clean bottle if you prefer.

VARIATION
If preferred, nectarines make a suitable and perhaps slightly more unusual replacement for peaches in this recipe.

INGREDIENTS

3 or 4 large, ripe, unblemished peaches

3½oz (100g) superfine sugar

1 vanilla bean, split lengthwise

2 cups brandy

EXTRA EQUIPMENT

½-gallon (2-liter) wide-necked glass jar

Choose slightly underripe peaches for this recipe and, for ease of preparation, purchase freestone, not the cling variety. Serve this delicious chutney with curries and cheese sandwiches.

Peach and ginger chutney

🕐 TAKES 40 MINUTES   🍲 MAKES 4½–5½LB (2–2.5KG)   🫙 KEEPS FOR UP TO 1 YEAR

1 Immerse the peaches in boiling water, then peel (see Peach and Pistachio Preserve, p62). Chop the flesh and discard the pits. Chop the onions. Crush the garlic and chiles, and finely grate the ginger.

2 Put the peach flesh, onion, garlic, and dried fruit in a heavy nonreactive pot. Stir in the chiles, ginger, and cider vinegar, then stir in the sugar.

3 Bring slowly to a boil over low heat, stirring occasionally. Once the sugar has dissolved, increase the heat and allow the chutney to simmer for 30–40 minutes until thick, stirring often and ensuring that the chutney at the bottom of the pan does not stick and burn.

4 Ladle the chutney into jars, cover with vinegar-proof seals, and label.

INGREDIENTS

3lb 3oz (1.5kg) peaches

2 large onions

6 garlic cloves

3 small dried red chiles

2in (5cm) piece of fresh ginger

1lb 2oz (500g) mixed dried fruit, such as raisins and apricots

4 cups cider vinegar

1½lb (675g) light brown or muscovado sugar

This softish relish goes well with grilled tuna, chicken kebabs, and hot dogs.

Nectarine and sweet corn relish

🕐 TAKES 45 MINUTES   🍲 MAKES 2¼LB (1KG)   🫙 KEEPS FOR 3 MONTHS

1 Cut the nectarines into ½in (1cm) cubes, discarding the pits. Chop the onions and chiles. Put all the ingredients except the sugar and salt in a large nonreactive pot, stir well, and bring to a boil. Cover and simmer for 10 minutes. Stir in the sugar and simmer for another 3–4 minutes until dissolved.

2 Increase the heat to medium and cook the relish for 20–30 minutes until most of the liquid has evaporated. Test to see whether the relish is ready (see p22). Stir in the salt.

3 Ladle the relish into hot sterilized jars, cover with vinegar-proof seals, and label. Use within 3 months.

INGREDIENTS

1lb 5oz (600g) nectarines

10oz (300g) red onions

1–2oz (30–60g) red jalapeño chile pepper

10oz (300g) sweet corn kernels

3 garlic cloves, crushed

1¾ cups white wine vinegar

1 tbsp fresh thyme leaves

7oz (200g) golden bakers' or regular white granulated sugar

2 tsp salt

A mix of fresh and dried apricots provides the basis for this spicy orange-colored relish. Serve it with chicken curries, chunks of bread and cheese, and in sandwiches.

Apricot and red onion relish

🕐 TAKES 50 MINUTES　　🍲 MAKES 4½LB (2KG)　　🫙 KEEPS FOR I YEAR

1　Put all the spices in a spice mill, and process until the mixture is finely ground. Alternatively, grind the spices using a mortar and pestle, sifting out any large pieces.

2　Put the garlic and ginger in a blender or food processor, and process to make a paste, or grind together with a mortar and pestle.

3　Put all the ingredients, including the ground spices and garlic-ginger paste, in a large nonreactive pot. Stir until thoroughly mixed. Simmer for 10 minutes, stirring occasionally, until the sugar has dissolved.

4　Increase the heat to medium and continue to simmer for 40 minutes, stirring occasionally, until it is thick and the fruit is cooked. Do keep an eye on the mixture toward the end of cooking, as it has a tendency to stick. The relish is ready when a wooden spoon dragged across the bottom of the pan leaves a clear path in the mixture.

5　Ladle the relish into hot sterilized jars, cover with vinegar-proof seals, and label. Store in a cool, dark place.

VARIATION
Any stone fruit works well in this recipe. Perhaps for ease I would choose nectarines as a substitute for apricots, as their thin skins make preparation of this relish a simple process.

INGREDIENTS

2 dried red chiles

2 dried bay leaves

2 tsp coriander seeds

I tsp allspice berries

I tsp black peppercorns

I tsp yellow mustard seeds

peeled cloves from I whole head of garlic

4in (10cm) piece of fresh ginger

2¼lb (1kg) fresh apricots, pitted and chopped

Ilb 2oz (500g) dried apricots, chopped

Ilb 10oz (750g) red onions, chopped

7oz (200g) chopped celery

I red bell pepper, seeded and chopped

I tbsp salt

3 cups white wine vinegar

Ilb 2oz (500g) Demerara or raw sugar, or golden baker's granulated sugar

This plum sauce is most often served with crispy duck, but it could also add a zing to many stir-fries. Away from the Chinese kitchen, I like to serve it with cold meats and cheeses. I also use it as a baste for pork roasts or chops toward the end of cooking, to give them extra flavor. Plums of any color may be used, making this recipe handy if you have an abundance of fruit.

Chinese plum sauce

🕐 TAKES 90 MINUTES   🍲 MAKES 4 CUPS   🥫 KEEPS FOR 1 YEAR

1   Cut the plums in half and remove the pits: this will make sieving easier later on. Put all the ingredients except the sugar and star anise in a large nonreactive pot. Bring to a boil, cover, and simmer for 20 minutes or until all the ingredients are very soft.

2   Press the mixture through a food mill or coarse sieve, and return to the cleaned pan.

3   Add the sugar and star anise, and bring back to a boil, stirring frequently to ensure that the sugar dissolves. Simmer the mixture for 30–60 minutes until the sauce is thick and creamy.

4   Ladle the plum sauce into hot sterilized bottles, seal with vinegar-proof lids, and label.

VARIATION

If you would like a more fiery sauce, add 4–6 red chile peppers, seeded if preferred, then chopped, with the vegetables at the start of cooking.

INGREDIENTS

4½lb (2kg) ripe plums

1lb 10oz (750g) white onions, chopped

peeled cloves from 1–2 whole heads of garlic, chopped

8in (20cm) piece of fresh ginger, about 14oz (400g), peeled and chopped

1 cup soy sauce

4 cups unseasoned rice wine vinegar

2¼lb (1kg) light brown or muscovado sugar

6 star anise seeds, finely ground

Ketchup doesn't need to be made with tomatoes—I always make mine with plums, a sort of upscale condiment. Full of flavor and sublimely spicy, this ketchup simply demands plump pork sausages and a mound of mashed potatoes or, better yet, eggs and fried potatoes.

Spicy plum ketchup

🕐 TAKES 1–1¼ HOURS   🍲 MAKES 4 CUPS   🗄 KEEPS FOR 12–18 MONTHS

1 Halve and pit the plums, and chop if large. Put in a large nonreactive pot with the dates, raisins, onion, garlic, and ginger. Add the ground coriander seeds, allspice, cayenne, and 2 cups of the vinegar.

2 Bring the mixture to a boil, then simmer for 30–40 minutes until the fruit is very soft.

3 Let the mixture cool, then press through a food mill or sieve.

4 Return the purée to the cleaned pot. Add the remaining vinegar, turmeric, nutmeg, sugar, and salt. Bring the mixture to a boil. Simmer for 30–45 minutes until reduced to a thick, pouring consistency, stirring frequently.

5 Let the ketchup cool, then transfer to hot sterilized jars or bottles, cover with vinegar-proof seals, and label. Store in a cool, dark place for at least a month before using.

VARIATION

If you have a favorite combination of spices, why not experiment here? I sometimes add some celery seed. Dark muscovado sugar, instead of the light variety listed, adds a deeper flavor and one that is more suitable for adult tastes.

INGREDIENTS

4½lb (2kg) plums

6oz (175g) pitted dates, chopped

4oz (115g) raisins

1 large onion, chopped

4 plump garlic cloves, chopped

2in (5cm) piece of fresh ginger, about 2oz (60g), finely grated

1 tbsp freshly ground coriander seeds

1 tsp freshly ground allspice berries

good pinch of cayenne pepper

4 cups malt or wine vinegar

1 tbsp ground turmeric

½ nutmeg, freshly grated

10oz (300g) light brown or muscovado sugar

¼ cup salt

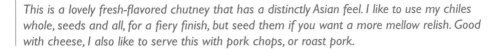

This is a lovely fresh-flavored chutney that has a distinctly Asian feel. I like to use my chiles whole, seeds and all, for a fiery finish, but seed them if you want a more mellow relish. Good with cheese, I also like to serve this with pork chops, or roast pork.

Red plum, lime, and coriander chutney

🕐 TAKES I HOUR   🍲 MAKES 4½LB (2KG)   🥫 KEEPS FOR I YEAR

1   In a spice mill or using a mortar and pestle, grind the cinnamon, coriander, and peppercorns together until you have a fine powder. Halve and pit the plums, then coarsely chop.

2   Put all the ingredients in a large nonreactive pot and slowly bring to a boil, stirring often to dissolve the sugar.

3   Once the sugar has dissolved, simmer gently for 50–60 minutes until the chutney is thick. Stir frequently toward the end of cooking to keep the mixture from sticking to the bottom of the pan and burning.

4   Once the chutney has reduced and thickened, turn off the heat and let it cool for 10 minutes.

5   Ladle into hot sterilized jars, cover with vinegar-proof seals, and label. Store in a cool, dark place for at least 1 month before using.

VARIATION

Star anise is a possible additional spice here, but, as it can be a bit overwhelming, the seeds from 1 or 2 stars, finely crushed, will suffice.

INGREDIENTS

6in (15cm) cinnamon stick

2 tbsp coriander seeds

1 tsp black peppercorns

4½lb (2kg) red plums

2 large onions, chopped

5 garlic cloves, chopped

2 red chiles, seeded for a milder flavor, if desired, and chopped

2in (5cm) piece of fresh ginger, about 2oz (60g), finely grated

finely grated zest and freshly squeezed juice of 2 limes

finely grated zest and freshly squeezed juice of 1 lemon

2 cups red wine vinegar

1lb 2oz (500g) Demerara or raw sugar, or light muscovado or brown sugar

Summer vegetables

Eggplant • Beets • Cabbage • Carrots • Cauliflower
Zucchini • Squash • Mushrooms • Onions • Pumpkin
Rhubarb • Tomatoes

With its affinity for sugar and spices, pumpkin lends itself to both savory and sweet treatments. Eating this flame-colored pumpkin butter is akin to tasting autumn. Spread it on buttered toast, eat it on gingerbread, or spoon it onto waffles and serve with whipped cream.

Spiced pumpkin butter

⏱ TAKES 1½ HOURS   🍲 MAKES 1½LB (1.6KG)   🥫 KEEPS FOR 6 MONTHS

1 Put the pumpkin in a steamer and steam for 10 minutes or until soft. Transfer to a blender or food processor, and process until you have a smooth purée.

2 Transfer the purée to a heavy nonreactive pot and add the sugar.

3 Using a clean coffee mill, grind the spices to a fine powder. Alternatively, grind using a mortar and pestle. Stir into the pumpkin purée along with the lemon juice and zest.

4 Simmer the butter over low heat for 60–90 minutes until very thick, stirring frequently. Take care, as the butter can spatter as it cooks. The mixture is quite thick to begin with, but needs long cooking to condense and form the butter.

5 When the purée is as thick as it can be (it will begin to stick to the bottom of the pot no matter how often you stir) and when a wooden spoon drawn across the bottom of the pan leaves a clear path, it is ready. Ladle it into hot sterilized jars, seal, and label.

INGREDIENTS

4½lb (2kg) pumpkin, peeled, seeded and cut into ¾in (2cm) cubes

1lb 5oz (600g) unrefined (raw) sugar

1 cinnamon stick, broken into pieces

½ of a whole nutmeg

6 cloves

2 shavings of mace taken from the outside of a whole nutmeg

finely grated zest and freshly squeezed juice of 2 lemons

COOKING IN A STEAMER

Pumpkin has a high water content, so steaming this fruit rather than boiling it in water prevents the pumpkin from disintegrating into mush, preserves more of its vitamin content, and retains more of its flavor. For even cooking, cut into even-sized cubes.

This is a really old-fashioned jam, once made by our mothers and grandmothers. It is still worth thinking about if you have a large ripe squash left at the end of the summer. Fresh ginger adds the necessary edge to an otherwise subtle flavor.

Zucchini and ginger jam

⏱ TAKES 25 MINUTES   🍲 MAKES 2¼LB (1KG)   🥫 KEEPS FOR 6 MONTHS

1   Layer the zucchini in a large china or glass bowl, sprinkling each layer with sugar and lemon juice, until all the sugar and juice has been used. Set aside for 24 hours.

2   Drain the liquid from the zucchini. Transfer the liquid to a heavy nonreactive pot, along with any remaining undissolved sugar.

3   Add the lemon zest and ginger to the pan, and bring the mixture to a boil. Boil rapidly for about 20 minutes until the liquid is reduced by roughly half.

4   Add the zucchini cubes, and simmer for another 4–5 minutes until the zucchini is soft. Skim off any scum from the surface of the jam.

5   Add the pectin and cook at a full rolling boil for 2 minutes, then test for a set.

6   Once the jam has reached the setting point, let it stand for up to 20 minutes or until the zucchini pieces have settled, then ladle into hot sterilized jars, seal, and label.

INGREDIENTS

3lb 3oz (1.5kg) zucchini or other summer squash flesh, peeled, seeded and cut into ¾in (2cm) cubes

2¼lb (1kg) granulated sugar

finely grated zest and freshly squeezed juice of 3 lemons, about ½ cup

4oz (115g) fresh ginger, peeled and grated

9oz (250g) liquid pectin

Naturally sour, rhubarb has a wonderful taste that comes alive with the addition of sugar. While it contains much acid, rhubarb has little pectin, so you will need to add this to achieve a set. Given rhubarb's high acidity, avoid aluminum saucepans in making this recipe.

Rhubarb marmalade

🕐 TAKES 20 MINUTES　　🍲 MAKES 3LB (1.35KG)　　🫙 KEEPS FOR 6 MONTHS

1　Put the rhubarb, sugar, juice, and zest into a heavy nonreactive pot. Bring the mixture slowly to a boil, then simmer over low heat for 5–8 minutes until the rhubarb is soft and the sugar has dissolved.

2　Now add the pectin and mix in gently, stirring until well blended. Return the marmalade to a boil, and cook for another 2 minutes before testing for a set.

3　Once the marmalade has reached the setting point, ladle into hot sterilized jars, seal, and label.

VARIATION

Rhubarb has a particular affinity with ginger, so try adding a little grated fresh ginger to this recipe to give it a spicy lift.

INGREDIENTS

2¼lb (1kg) rhubarb, washed and cut into ½in (1cm) lengths

1¾lb (800g) granulated sugar

finely grated zest and freshly squeezed juice of 2 oranges

4½oz (125g) liquid pectin

Carrot makes a bold-colored jam and spicing it with cardamom seeds adds an exotic feel to this preserve. To find the seeds, split open the green cardamom pods and discard them: the seeds lay tucked inside. Serve this spicy jam with whole-wheat toast and Cheddar cheese.

Carrot and cardamom jam

🕐 TAKES 25 MINUTES   🍲 MAKES 3LB (1.5KG)   🫙 KEEPS FOR 1 YEAR

1 Put the carrots in a saucepan, cover with water, and boil for 10–15 minutes until tender. Drain the carrots and chop them finely.

2 Put the carrots, lemon, orange zests and juices, and cardamom seeds in a heavy pot. Add the sugar, and cook over low heat until the sugar has dissolved.

3 Increase the heat and boil the mixture for 5 minutes.

4 Add the pectin, return the mixture to a boil, and cook for another 2 minutes. Test for a set.

5 Once the jam has reached the setting point, leave to cool for another 10 minutes, then stir to distribute the carrot and cardamom. Ladle into hot sterilized jars, seal, and label.

VARIATION
Very young parsnips, tough cores removed, also have the necessary sweetness to make a tasty and unusual jam. They should be used as soon as possible after purchase to ensure the best possible finished preserve.

INGREDIENTS

1lb 2oz (500g) fresh young carrots, peeled and cut into ¾in (2cm) lengths

finely grated zest of 2 lemons

freshly squeezed juice of 3 lemons

finely grated zest and freshly squeezed juice of 1 large orange

1 tbsp cardamom seeds

2¼lb (1kg) granulated sugar

4½oz (125g) liquid pectin

This chutney reminds me of warm Mediterranean sunshine and summer holidays. Eggplant and orange work well together. I use fresh-tasting green chiles in this recipe, but fiery red ones could replace them. Serve the relish with grilled lamb kebabs and meat or fish stews.

Eggplant, orange, and coriander chutney

TAKES 60 MINUTES   MAKES 3¾LB (1.7KG)   KEEPS FOR UP TO 1 YEAR

1   Put the spices in a clean coffee mill and process until coarsely ground. Alternatively, grind with a mortar and pestle.

2   Put the ground spices and the remaining ingredients in a heavy nonreactive pot. Cook over low heat, stirring occasionally to dissolve the sugar.

3   Increase the heat and bring the mixture to a boil. Simmer for 1 hour, stirring occasionally, until the chutney is very thick. Keep an eye on the mixture as it cooks, because this particular chutney has a tendency to stick and burn.

4   When the mixture has reached the desired consistency—you should be able to make a clear path with a wooden spoon across the bottom of the pan—ladle the chutney into hot sterilized jars, cover with vinegar-proof seals, and label. Store in a cool, dark place.

VARIATION

You can vary the spices used here to suit your taste—fennel seeds work well, as does freshly grated ginger.

INGREDIENTS

2 tbsp coriander seeds

1 tbsp cumin seeds

½ teaspoon black peppercorns

2¼lb (1kg) eggplant, trimmed and cut into ½in (1cm) dice

1lb 2oz (600g) red onions, chopped

4 fresh green chiles, seeded if desired, and chopped

4–6 plump garlic cloves, crushed

finely grated zest and freshly squeezed juice of 2 large oranges

2⅓ cups cider vinegar

14oz (400g) Demerara or raw sugar

1 tbsp salt

Zucchini might not be the first vegetable that comes to mind when thinking of chutney-making, but a glut of this flavorful squash is just what's needed to make this tangy pickle, spiced with ginger, mustard, and coriander. I like to serve it with sausage and mashed potatoes.

Chunky zucchini chutney

TAKES 35 MINUTES   MAKES 4LB (1.8KG)   KEEPS FOR UP TO 1 YEAR

1   Combine all the ingredients except the sugar, salt, and dill in a large nonreactive pot. Bring the mixture to a boil, then reduce the heat to medium and simmer gently for 10–15 minutes until the vegetables begin to soften.

2   Add the sugar and salt, and continue to simmer for another 15 minutes or so, until most of the liquid has evaporated.

3   Add the dill, and simmer for 2–3 minutes until the chutney has reached the desired consistency.

4   Ladle into hot sterilized jars, seal, and label.

VARIATION
Zucchini of all colors can be used in this recipe, including white or yellow patty pan, round green ball zucchini, and the newer black varieties.

INGREDIENTS

2¼lb (1kg) firm medium zucchini, quartered lengthwise and cut into ½in (1cm) dice

4 large red onions, cut into ½in (1cm) dice

3 plump garlic cloves, crushed

2½oz (75g) fresh ginger, finely chopped

2 tsp black mustard seeds

1 tbsp coarsely ground coriander seeds

2 cups cider vinegar

7oz (200g) golden raisins (sultanas)

12oz (350g) granulated sugar

1 tbsp salt

¼ cup fresh dill or fennel

Preserving tomatoes

MAKING THE MOST OF THE CROP

The delight of growing your own tomatoes is harvesting them, sweet and fresh, from the living plants in your garden—or, failing that, buying freshly picked ones from farmers' markets. Warehouse-ripened tomatoes cannot compare. Life is never that simple, though, and I often find that I have a mass of green, ripe, and overripe tomatoes all at the same time. Fortunately there are recipes that perfectly suit each stage of ripeness. All varieties can be used—look for the most plentiful crops.

Green tomatoes

A glut of green tomatoes gives you the perfect opportunity to stir up a batch of sharp and spicy green tomato chutney. These tomatoes have a higher than average acid content and are highly flavored, but without the balancing sweetness of riper fruits. Look for mature, full-sized tomatoes that are beginning to turn slightly orange. Immature vine tomatoes are unsuitable for pickling, however, as they are not fully developed.

GREEN TOMATOES

RIPE TOMATOES

Ripe tomatoes

Use ripe tomatoes for lightly cooked, chunky tomato relishes. Look for firm flesh, good aroma, and a wonderful depth of color. Ripeness can be detected by smell, feel, and taste, but don't be misled by the scent of the calyx: this is not an indication of flavor.

Overripe tomatoes

With their heady sweetness, overripe tomatoes make wonderful sauces and ketchups. Vinegar replaces their lost acidity. Do not confuse them with rotten fruits, which smell harsh and have almost liquid flesh, and avoid any with mold.

OVERRIPE TOMATOES

Why relish and not chutney? Well, this side dish is lightly cooked to thicken it and, while it keeps well for 2–3 months if stored in the refrigerator, it doesn't have enough sugar or vinegar to be stored on the pantry shelf. The good news is that, unlike long-keeping chutneys that need time to mature, this relish is ready to serve at once.

Tomato and fennel hamburger relish

🕐 TAKES 20 MINUTES 🍲 MAKES 1½LB (750G) 🫙 KEEPS FOR 2–3 MONTHS

1 Heat the oil in a heavy nonreactive pot, add the onion and garlic, and cook over low heat until softened.

2 Meanwhile, prepare the tomatoes. I leave the skins on for a chunky relish, but if you have a real aversion to the skins, go ahead and peel them. To do this, score the tomatoes lightly on the base and immerse in a bowl of boiling water for a few seconds until the skins begin to loosen. Drain, return to the bowl, and cover with cold water to cool, then peel using a sharp knife.

3 Cut the tomatoes into ½in (1cm) dice, removing any tough or stringy cores. Add to the saucepan along with the sugar, vinegar, fennel seeds, salt, and pepper. Cook over medium heat for 5–7 minutes until the mixture has thickened (it will thicken more as it cools).

4 Remove from the heat, and stir in the chopped herb. Ladle the relish into hot sterilized jars, seal with vinegar-proof lids, and label. Store in the refrigerator.

VARIATION
Instead of fennel, try coriander or mustard seeds—but remember that mustard seeds will add heat as well as flavor to the finished relish.

INGREDIENTS

2 tbsp olive oil

1 large red onion, chopped

2 plump garlic cloves, crushed

1lb 2oz (500g) ripe tomatoes

3 tbsp muscovado or light brown sugar

3 tbsp white wine vinegar

1 tsp fennel seeds, crushed

1 tsp salt

a good quantity of freshly ground black pepper

2–3 tbsp chopped fresh cilantro, tarragon, or basil

Look for tiny cherry tomatoes for this relish and make sure they are just underripe. As always, the amount of chile used is up to you. I have used only a small quantity, as this relish is a favorite with children. For a hotter, more fiery mix, increase the number of chiles and leave the seeds in, if desired. Serve with hamburgers, sausages, and kebabs.

Cherry tomato and onion relish

🕐 TAKES 1 HOUR   🍲 MAKES 4LB (1.8KG)   🫙 KEEPS FOR 6–9 MONTHS

1 Put the onions, chile, and garlic in a nonreactive pot. Add the celery seed and vinegar and bring the mixture to a boil. Simmer for 15–20 minutes until the vegetables are cooked and most of the liquid has evaporated.

2 Add the tomatoes. Stir in the sugar and return to a boil. Simmer the relish over medium heat for 30 minutes or until the tomatoes soften and the relish thickens.

3 Remove from the heat and stir in the chopped basil.

4 Ladle the relish into hot sterilized jars, cover with vinegar-proof seals, and label.

VARIATION

Although I have used white sugar because it gives a better flavor to this relish, raw brown sugar can be used instead. You can also vary the flavoring, using fennel seeds instead of celery seed, and chopped fresh mint in place of the basil.

INGREDIENTS

2¼lb (1kg) onions, chopped

1 fresh green chile, seeded if desired, and chopped

4 plump garlic cloves, crushed

1 tbsp celery seed

14fl oz (400ml) cider vinegar

2¼lb (1kg) cherry tomatoes, quartered if large

9oz (250g) granulated sugar

good handful of chopped fresh basil

Rather more tasty and definitely less sweet than the commercial varieties, this family favorite can be made even more spicy with the addition of hot pepper sauce. If I have no ripe tomatoes on hand, I simply use good-quality Italian canned plum tomatoes instead.

Tomato ketchup

🕐 TAKES 35 MINUTES   🥘 MAKES 5LB (2.25KG)   🫙 KEEPS FOR 6 MONTHS

1 For the spice mix, put all the ingredients in a clean coffee mill and process until reduced to a powder, or grind using a mortar and pestle.

2 Put the tomatoes, onions, garlic, pepper, and celery in a large saucepan. Cover and cook gently over medium heat for about 15 minutes until all the ingredients are very soft. Pass the mixture through a fine sieve or food mill.

3 Return the purée to the cleaned pan, and add the sugar, vinegar, and finely ground spice mix. Simmer for 20 minutes, stirring frequently, until the mixture thickens.

4 Remove from the heat and add the hot pepper sauce, if using. Ladle into hot sterilized jars or bottles, seal with vinegar-proof lids, and label.

INGREDIENTS

6½lb (3kg) very ripe tomatoes

1lb 2oz (500g) onions, chopped

8 plump garlic cloves

1 large red bell pepper, seeded and chopped

7oz (200g) celery, chopped

8oz (225g) granulated sugar

8fl oz (250ml) cider vinegar

½–1 tsp hot pepper sauce, such as Tabasco (optional)

FOR THE SPICE MIX

15 cloves

20 allspice berries

1 tsp celery seed

4in (10cm) cinnamon stick, broken into pieces

1 tbsp salt

1 tsp black peppercorns

VARYING THE CONSISTENCY

Thick or thin ketchup—the choice is yours. Vary the cooking time to achieve the consistency you like. You can also vary the spices according to what you enjoy. Coriander seed could replace the celery seed, while dark brown muscovado sugar would deepen the flavor.

At summer's end, I always have plenty of green tomatoes that seem resistant to ripening. This recipe makes such good use of them that it has become one of my pantry essentials. Serve this chutney with cheese, cold ham, and hot sausages.

Green tomato chutney

(L) TAKES 1¼ HOURS ⌣ MAKES 5LB (2.5KG) ⊟ KEEPS FOR 6–9 MONTHS

1 Put the tomatoes, onions, and apples in a heavy nonreactive pot with the vinegar. Simmer for about 30 minutes until the vegetables and apples are soft.

2 Meanwhile, prepare the chiles, removing the seeds, if desired, for a milder flavor. Transfer the chiles to a blender or food processor with the garlic and ginger, and process to a smooth paste.

3 Add the paste to the pan with the raisins, sugar, and salt. Simmer over low heat for 5 minutes, stirring, until the sugar has dissolved.

4 Increase the heat to medium, and continue to cook the chutney for 30–40 minutes until thick.

5 Ladle into hot sterilized jars, cover with vinegar-proof seals, and label.

INGREDIENTS

4½lb (2kg) green tomatoes, cores removed and sliced

1lb 10oz (750g) onions, chopped

1lb 2oz (500g) cooking apples, cored and finely chopped

2⅓ cups cider vinegar

4–6 red chiles, or to taste

6 plump garlic cloves

1oz (30g) fresh ginger

8oz (225g) golden raisins (sultanas)

1lb 2oz (500g) granulated sugar

2 tsp salt

CONTRASTING TEXTURES

Try to find large green tomatoes for this recipe—these give the best ratio of flesh to skin and seeds. Just-underripe ones also work well. Apples provide necessary bulk. Both these and the tomatoes will cook down, but the raisins retain their shape, adding extra flavor and texture.

A bright addition to any table, this relish is simple to make and looks wonderful. Try to use small beets for their intense flavor. Serve with pork, burgers, or cheese, especially Cheddar.

Beet and orange relish

🕐 TAKES 1½ HOURS   🍲 MAKES 5LB (2.25KG)   🫙 KEEPS FOR UP TO 1 YEAR

1 Peel the beets and grate coarsely. This can be a messy procedure and the juice will stain both your hands and the chopping board, so it is best done in a food processor fitted with the grating disk. If grating the beets by hand, cover the work surface with a layer of newspaper, and wear rubber gloves to protect your hands.

2 Grate the zest from the oranges and set aside. Using a sharp knife, cut away all the white pith from the fruit. Cut the fruit into small dice, removing any seeds and excess coarse membrane as you do.

3 For the spice mix, finely grind the cloves, cinnamon, allspice berries, and coriander seeds together in a spice mill or clean coffee grinder.

4 Put all the ingredients in a large nonreactive pot. Bring to a boil, stirring often to ensure that the sugar dissolves.

5 Reduce the heat and simmer for up to 1½ hours until the relish thickens, stirring frequently and taking care not to let the mixture stick and burn.

6 Ladle into hot sterilized jars, seal with vinegar-proof lids, and label.

VARIATION
Using a muscovado or brown sugar, light or dark, instead of the white sugar will give a deeper flavor to the finished relish.

INGREDIENTS

2¼lb (1kg) beets

4 large, thick-skinned oranges

8 cloves

4in (10cm) cinnamon stick

20 allspice berries

1 tbsp coriander seeds

3 large onions, finely chopped

2in (5cm) piece of fresh ginger, about 2oz (60g), grated

4 plump garlic cloves, crushed

1lb 5oz (600g) granulated sugar

2 cups red wine vinegar

1 tbsp salt

This relish contains oil and so does not keep as well as other chutneys. Store in the refrigerator and use within two months. Serve with steak sandwiches, sausages, and pork dishes.

Onion marmalade

🕐 TAKES I HOUR   🍲 MAKES I LB 5OZ (600G)   🥫 KEEPS FOR 2 MONTHS

1   Heat the oil in a large, deep frying pan and add the onions. Cook over low heat for 35–40 minutes, stirring frequently, until the onions have reduced considerably and are very soft. It is important not to allow the onions to brown, or the flavor of the marmalade will be too strong.

2   Once the onions have reduced, add the salt, sugar, vinegar, and thyme. Simmer until most of the liquid has evaporated and the marmalade is thick. Ladle into hot sterilized jars, cover with vinegar-proof seals, and label. Store in the refrigerator.

INGREDIENTS

1¾lb (800g) red onions, thinly sliced

¼ cup olive oil

I tsp salt

3½oz (100g) granulated sugar

5 tbsp red wine vinegar

I tbsp fresh thyme leaves

Balsamic vinegar adds its characteristic sweetness to white wine vinegar in this unusual pickle.

Pickled garlic in balsamic vinegar

🕐 TAKES 10 MINUTES   🍲 MAKES I LB (450G)   🥫 KEEPS FOR 6 MONTHS

1   Put the vinegars, sugar, salt, bay leaf, and spices in a saucepan over low heat, and simmer for a few minutes until the sugar has dissolved.

2   Separate the garlic into cloves, peel, and add to the pan. Increase the heat and boil for 5 minutes. Drain, reserving the spiced vinegar.

3   Pack the garlic into hot sterilized jars. Pour in the vinegar, ensuring that the spices are evenly distributed and the garlic is covered: add more vinegar if necessary. Seal with vinegar-proof lids and label. Store in a cool, dark place for I month before using. These garlic cloves sometimes form small brown spots on the surface, as do pickled onions, but the pickle is still edible.

INGREDIENTS

2 cups white wine vinegar

¼ cup balsamic vinegar

2oz (60g) sugar

I tsp salt

I bay leaf

½ tsp coriander seeds

½ tsp white peppercorns

2–3 small dried red chiles

2–3 heads of garlic

Homemade pickled onions are far superior to ready-made ones, so settle down, switch on the radio, and get peeling. Choose small onions and buy them as soon as you see them—these tiny onions usually appear in markets for only a few brief weeks.

Pickled onions

⏱ NO COOKING   🍲 MAKES 2¼LB (1KG)   🥫 KEEPS FOR UP TO 1 YEAR

1   For the brine, put the salt in a large heatproof china or glass bowl. Pour in 10fl oz (300ml) boiling water, and stir to dissolve the salt. Add another 4 cups cold water.

2   To make the onions easier to peel, bring a saucepan of water to a boil, then remove from the heat, add the onions, and let sit for a few seconds. Taking one onion at a time, cut away the tops and roots, and remove and discard all the brown outer skin. Immediately immerse the peeled onion in the brine. As the onions are best peeled hot, you may need to pop the pan and its contents back on the heat for a few minutes if the skins become resistant.

3   Set the onions aside for 24 hours, to steep in the brine.

4   Make the spiced vinegar. Put the vinegar and spices in a saucepan, stir, and cook over low heat until heated through, about 3–4 minutes. The vinegar does not need to boil. Cover and set aside.

5   Drain the brined onions and wash well under cold running water. Pat dry using a clean dish towel or paper towels.

6   Pack the onions into cold sterilized jars, then pour in the spiced vinegar, ensuring that the onions are completely covered and adding more vinegar if required. I usually add some extra spices to each jar.

7   Seal with vinegar-proof lids, and store the onions in a cool, dark place. Check the onions after a couple of days to make sure they are still submerged in the vinegar. If necessary, add a bit of plain malt vinegar. Let sit for at least 1 month before using.

INGREDIENTS

8oz (225g) salt

2¼lb (1kg) pickling onions

FOR THE SPICED VINEGAR

4 cups malt vinegar, plus extra if needed

1 bay leaf

6 cloves

2–3 shavings of mace, taken from the outside of a whole nutmeg

12 allspice berries

1 tbsp black peppercorns

1–2 dried red chiles (optional)

Pork pie without piccalilli; ploughman's lunch without piccalilli? Unthinkable! This is a classic pickle and a real favorite, and one that really is better homemade. Serve it with good hearty simple fare, such as grilled sausages, or cold meats and firm cheeses with crusty bread.

Piccalilli

🕐 TAKES 10 MINUTES   🍲 MAKES 4½LB (2KG)   🥫 KEEPS FOR 6 MONTHS

1   For the brine, put the salt in a large heatproof china or glass bowl. Pour in 15fl oz (450ml) boiling water and stir to dissolve the salt. Add another 6 cups cold water. Add the vegetables and let sit overnight.

2   For the sauce, combine the flour, mustard, sugar, and turmeric in a large bowl. Add a little of the vinegar and work into a paste, adding more vinegar if required. Mix in the remaining vinegar, and pour into a large nonreactive pot.

3   Bring the mixture to a boil, whisking constantly for a smooth, thick sauce. Simmer for 4–5 minutes until the sauce is thick and smooth, continuing to whisk. Remove from the heat.

4   Rinse the vegetables and drain well. Add all the vegetables to the sauce, return to a boil, and simmer for about 3 minutes until they are cooked but still a little crisp.

5   Ladle into hot sterilized jars, pressing the vegetables down to ensure that they are covered and adding extra vinegar if needed. Seal with vinegar-proof lids, and label.

VARIATION

This mixed vegetable pickle offers an excellent way to make the most of late summer's bounty. Cauliflower and pickling onions are essential ingredients, but some people also include carrots.

INGREDIENTS

8oz (225g) salt

1lb (450g) pickling onions

1 medium cauliflower, broken into small florets

8oz (225g) runner beans, sliced into 1in (2.5cm) lengths

2 cucumbers or zucchini, seeded and diced

2 heads of plump garlic cloves

FOR THE SAUCE

1oz (30g) all-purpose flour

2oz (60g) mustard powder

8oz (225g) granulated sugar

1 tbsp ground turmeric

3 cups distilled vinegar, plus extra if needed

This rich brown pickle is almost but not quite a chutney. It has a mix of vegetables and is lightly cooked in a rich sweet and spicy sauce. It's perfect with crusty bread and cheese, but good, too, with cold meats and in sandwiches.

Ploughman's pickle

🕐 TAKES 30 MINUTES   🍲 MAKES 8LB (3.6KG)   🥫 KEEPS FOR 6 MONTHS

1 For the brine, put the salt in a large heatproof china or glass bowl. Pour in 10fl oz (300ml) boiling water and stir to dissolve the salt. Add another 5 cups cold water.

2 Put the vegetables in a large glass or china bowl, pour in the brine, and let sit overnight.

3 The following morning, drain the vegetables and rinse well under cold running water. Lay on a clean dish towel to drain.

4 Meanwhile, put the apples and garlic in a large nonreactive pot with 1¼ cups of the vinegar. Simmer for 10 minutes or until soft. Remove from the heat.

5 In a bowl, mix the cornstarch with about ¼ cup of the vinegar into a smooth paste, and set aside.

6 Add the remaining vinegar, sugar, and spices to the pan, including the cayenne, if using. Bring the mixture to a boil, stirring until the sugar dissolves. Stir a few spoonfuls of the hot liquid into the cornstarch mixture, then add to the pan. Stir constantly while the mixture thickens until you have a smooth sauce.

7 Simmer for 2–3 minutes, then add the drained vegetables. Bring to a boil, then simmer for 5 minutes. Take care with this pickle, as it burns easily.

8 Ladle into hot sterilized jars, seal with vinegar-proof lids, and label.

INGREDIENTS

8oz (225g) salt

1 large cauliflower, broken into florets

1lb 10oz (750g) firm zucchini, cut into ½in (1cm) dice

2 large onions, cut into ½in (1cm) dice

1 celery heart, cut into ½in (1cm) dice

1lb (450g) cooking apples, cored and diced

4 or 5 plump garlic cloves, crushed

4 cups distilled vinegar

2oz (60g) cornstarch

1½lb (675g) dark brown or muscovado sugar

1 tbsp ground cinnamon

1 tbsp ground turmeric

1 tbsp ground cumin

1 tsp ground nutmeg

1 tsp allspice

¼ tsp cayenne pepper (optional)

To avoid diluting the concentration of vinegar in this pickle, the cucumbers must be drained of their excess liquid. Salting rather than brining is used here, as the water content of the cucumbers is high. Eat with hot dogs, hamburgers, and deli sandwiches.

Bread and butter pickle

⏱ TAKES 15 MINUTES   🥘 MAKES 2¼LB (1KG)   🥫 KEEPS FOR UP TO 3 MONTHS

1   Arrange the vegetables in a shallow bowl and sprinkle with the salt. Toss lightly with a fork to coat. Let sit overnight.

2   The following morning, drain the vegetables, rinse under cold running water, then spread out on clean dish towels to drain.

3   In a large nonreactive pot or stainless-steel saucepan, combine the vinegar, sugar, and spices. Bring this mixture to a boil, then simmer for 10 minutes.

4   Add the drained vegetables and boil for 1 minute. Remove with a slotted spoon.

5   Pack the vegetables into hot sterilized jars, and pour in the hot pickling liquid. Make sure that the vegetables are completely immersed in the liquid, adding extra vinegar if needed. Seal with vinegar-proof lids and label. Store in a cool, dark place. Once opened, store in the refrigerator.

INGREDIENTS

2 large or 4–6 small cucumbers, seeded if large, and thinly sliced

1 green bell pepper, seeded and thinly sliced

1 large mild onion, thinly sliced

1¾oz (50g) salt

14fl oz (400ml) cider vinegar, plus extra if needed

7oz (200g) granulated sugar

1 tsp ground turmeric

1 tsp celery seed, coarsely crushed

1 tsp mustard powder

1 tsp fennel seeds, coarsely crushed

CAREFUL PREPARATION

Look for firm cucumbers and choose ones that are on the small side, as these will contain less water. When preparing the cucumbers, pepper, and onion, try to cut everything evenly and thinly. The finished pickle will benefit from this extra care, making it well worth the time and effort.

This is a cabbage pickle that can be made in a dozen different ways. I like to salt the vegetables, then cook them in the seasoned vinegar. You can make up your own spice mix by adding fennel, dill, coriander seeds, or finely grated ginger.

Chow chow

🕐 TAKES 20 MINUTES   🍲 MAKES 4½LB (2KG)   🗄 KEEPS FOR 3–6 MONTHS

1 In a large china or glass bowl, arrange the vegetables in layers, sprinkling each layer with salt. Cover with a dry cloth and let sit in a cold place for 12 hours.

2 Drain the vegetables and rinse well under cold running water. Spread out on a clean dry dish towel to drain.

3 Put the vegetables, vinegar, sugar, and spices in a large nonreactive pot. Bring the mixture to a boil, then reduce heat and simmer for 20 minutes.

4 Pack into hot sterilized jars, packing the mixture down firmly with a teaspoon. Seal with vinegar-proof lids, and label. Store in the refrigerator. The chow chow will be ready to eat after 1 week.

VARIATION
Grated carrot, red bell pepper, or even a small quantity of shredded red cabbage could be used to make a more colorful pickle.

INGREDIENTS

2¼lb (1kg) shredded white cabbage

1lb 5oz (600g) mild white onions

2 green bell peppers, thinly sliced

2oz (60g) salt

4 cups white wine vinegar

3½oz (100g) granulated sugar

3 tbsp black mustard seeds, lightly crushed

2 tbsp celery or dill seeds, lightly crushed

This pickle is flavored with curry seasonings, rather than curried as. I use a spoonful or two of store-bought curry paste, but you could use curry powder or your own masala blend. Work the powder into a paste with a little vinegar and the sugar before adding the remaining liquid.

Curried cauliflower and carrot pickle

🕐 TAKES 30–40 MINUTES 🍲 MAKES 3LB 3OZ (1.5KG) 🥫 KEEPS FOR 6 MONTHS

1 For the brine, combine the salt with 4 cups very cold water in a large bowl or pitcher.

2 Put the vegetables in a large glass or china bowl. Pour in the brine, cover, and let sit in a cool place for at least 6 hours or preferably overnight.

3 Drain and rinse well under cold running water. Spread the vegetables out on a clean dish towel to dry.

4 Combine the vinegar, sugar, and curry paste or powder in a large nonreactive pot. Add the bay leaves and bring to a boil. Add the drained vegetables and simmer the mixture for 10–15 minutes. The vegetables should still retain some crispness. Drain the vegetables, reserving the spiced vinegar.

5 Pack the vegetables into hot sterilized wide-mouthed jars, and spoon in the vinegar, ensuring that the vegetables are covered, and adding extra vinegar if necessary.

6 Seal with vinegar-proof lids and label. Store in a cool, dark place. The pickle will be ready to eat after 4 weeks. The spices may sink to the bottom, so gently invert the jars before use.

INGREDIENTS

1½oz (45g) salt

1lb 10oz (750g) small cauliflower florets

1lb 2oz (500g) carrots, sliced

3½oz (100g) onion, thinly sliced

4 cups distilled malt vinegar, plus extra if needed

4½oz (125g) granulated sugar

1–2 tbsp curry paste or powder

2 bay leaves

These mushrooms are crisp, sweet, and salty, and excellent as an antipasto. Buy small, whole mushrooms and prepare as soon as possible. Remember that mushrooms soak up water like sponges; don't wash them, but rather brush them with a soft brush or dust with paper towels.

Pickled mushrooms

⏱ TAKES 25 MINUTES　　🍲 MAKES 2LB (900G)　　🫙 KEEPS FOR 3 MONTHS

1　Put all the ingredients except the mushrooms in a nonreactive pot and stir to combine. Bring to a boil, then reduce the heat and simmer over medium heat for 5 minutes.

2　Add the mushrooms to the pot and bring to a boil. Boil gently for 10 minutes longer.

3　Using a slotted spoon, remove the mushroom mixture from the pan, reserving the pickling liquid. Pack the mixture into hot sterilized jars.

4　Continue to boil the pickling liquid for 5–10 minutes until it has reduced by one-third. Pour over the mushrooms, ensuring that they are completely covered. Use extra vinegar if needed.

5　Seal with vinegar-proof lids, label, and store in the refrigerator.

VARIATION

If you collect wild mushrooms, they can be preserved in this fashion. Do be certain, though, that all the fungi are edible—mistakes can be unpleasant or even toxic. Use a reputable identification guide, or ask an expert. Clean wild mushrooms carefully, as they often contain grit, as well as tiny wildlife.

INGREDIENTS

2 cups white wine vinegar, plus extra if needed

2 garlic cloves, sliced

1 medium shallot, sliced

1 tbsp coriander seeds, coarsely crushed

1 tsp black peppercorns, coarsely crushed

1 tbsp dried oregano

1 tbsp granulated sugar

½ tsp salt

1½lb (750g) cultivated white mushrooms, trimmed

You can adapt this recipe for any quantity. If the beets are small, cut them into quarters. If large, I find slices work best. Beets will stain anything they comes into contact with, including your hands, so it is wise to wear rubber gloves when preparing.

Pickled beets

🕐 TAKES UP TO 1 HOUR   🍲 MAKES 4LB (1.8KG)   🥫 KEEPS FOR 6 MONTHS

1   Put the beets in a large nonreactive saucepan and cover with cold water. Bring to a boil, then simmer for 15 minutes for baby beets and up to 1 hour for larger ones, or until they are tender. Drain and set aside.

2   Meanwhile, in another nonreactive saucepan, combine the vinegar and all the spices except for the chiles, and bring to a boil. Turn off the heat and set aside.

3   As soon as the beets are cool enough to handle, slip off the skins. (I always wear gloves to do this, as the beets will stain your hands quite dramatically.) Quarter or slice the beets, and pack them into hot sterilized jars, slipping a chile or two down the sides if desired.

4   Strain the vinegar and pour over the beets. For a spicier pickle, don't strain the vinegar, but pour directly onto the beets, ensuring that the spices are evenly divided among the jars. The beets should be covered with vinegar, so add extra if necessary.

5   Seal with vinegar-proof lids, label, and store in a cool, dark place for 1 week before using.

VARIATION
Try adding some dill—either the crushed seeds or the fresh herb—to the vinegar in this recipe. Coriander combined with the finely grated zest of an orange also works well.

INGREDIENTS

2¼lb (1kg) beets, trimmed

4 cups distilled white or malt vinegar, plus extra if needed

2–3 shavings of mace from the outside of a nutmeg

1 cinnamon stick

1 bay leaf

1 tbsp black peppercorns

12 allspice berries

1–2 dried red chiles, or as needed (optional)

This rather old-fashioned pickle is still a favorite—and almost worth making for its beautiful color alone. My best memories of this pickle stem from my childhood. I can still picture the big bowls of salted cabbage waiting in our pantry for my mother to continue with the job.

Pickled red cabbage

🕐 TAKES 5–10 MINUTES   🍲 MAKES 4½LB (2KG)   🥫 KEEPS FOR UP TO 1 YEAR

1 Cut the cabbage in half and remove any coarse outer leaves. With a sharp knife, cut away the central core and discard. Slice the cabbage as thinly as possible.

2 Arrange the vegetables in alternating layers in a large china bowl, scattering the salt between the layers. Set aside and let sit overnight.

3 Meanwhile, pour the vinegar into a nonreactive saucepan and add the spices. Bring the mixture to a boil, stir in the sugar, then turn off the heat, cover the pan, and let sit overnight.

4 The following day, wash the cabbage and onion mixture under cold running water to remove all the salt. Drain in a colander, then spread on clean old dish towels to dry for about 1 hour.

5 Pack the cabbage into cold sterilized jars, pressing the cabbage down well. Pour in the vinegar, ensuring that each jar contains some of the spices and that the vinegar covers the vegetables. Top with extra vinegar if needed.

6 Seal with vinegar-proof lids, label, and store in a cool, dark place for at least 4 weeks before using.

INGREDIENTS

2¼ lb (1kg) red cabbage

2 red onions, thinly sliced

1–2 tbsp salt

FOR THE SPICED VINEGAR

4 cups distilled malt vinegar, plus extra if needed

3 shavings of mace, from the outside of a nutmeg, lightly crushed

1 cinnamon stick, lightly crushed

6 cloves, lightly crushed

12 allspice berries, lightly crushed

2–3 tbsp Demerara or raw sugar

If available, I like to include dill flowers in this pickle for their anise-like flavor. Pick them from the garden and add to the vinegar mix. Serve these beans with antipasti, or cold roast meats.

Pickled green beans with garlic

○ TAKES 20 MINUTES　　🍲 MAKES 2¼LB (1KG)　　🥫 KEEPS FOR 3–6 MONTHS

1　Trim the green beans and cut them in half. Chop the chile. Separate the garlic into cloves, and peel. Put all the ingredients except the beans in a nonreactive pot and bring to a boil. Simmer for 5 minutes. Add the beans and simmer for another 5 minutes.

2　Drain the mixture, reserving the vinegar, and spoon into hot sterilized jars.

3　Return the vinegar to the heat, and boil for 10 minutes or until reduced by about one-third. Pour over the beans, making sure that they are completely covered and adding extra vinegar if needed.

4　Seal with vinegar-proof lids, and label. Store in a cool, dark place. Once opened, store in the refrigerator.

INGREDIENTS

1¼lb (600g) green beans

1 dried red chile

1–2 heads of garlic

4 cups distilled malt vinegar

1 tsp salt

1¾oz (50g) granulated sugar

1 tsp coriander seeds

1 tbsp allspice berries

2–4 bay leaves

This may also be made with tiny pickling onions. Allow to mature for 4 weeks before using.

Sweet chile pickled shallots

○ NO COOKING　　🍲 MAKES 2LB (900G)　　🥫 KEEPS FOR UP TO 1 YEAR

1　For the brine, put the salt in a large heatproof china or glass bowl. Pour in 1¼ cups boiling water and stir to dissolve the salt. Add another 4 cups cold water.

2　Meanwhile, place the shallots in a bowl and cover with boiling water. Let sit for 5 minutes, then drain and peel. Separate the garlic into cloves; peel. Let the shallots and garlic sit in the brine overnight.

3　Crush the chiles. Heat the vinegar, sugar, bay leaves, and chiles in a nonreactive saucepan, then let sit overnight to infuse.

4　Drain and rinse the shallots and garlic. Pack into hot sterilized jars, pour in the vinegar, seal with vinegar-proof lids, and label.

INGREDIENTS

8oz (225g) salt

2¼lb (1kg) shallots

1 head of garlic

4 dried red chiles

4 cups distilled malt vinegar

3 tbsp light brown or muscovado sugar

3 bay leaves, crushed

These tangy little cucumbers are good with pâtés, cold meats, and sandwiches. They can also be chopped into mayonnaise-based sauces such as tartar sauce.

Pickled gherkins

🕐 TAKES 15 MINUTES   🍲 MAKES 1LB 10OZ (750G)   🥫 KEEPS FOR 6–9 MONTHS

1   For the brine, dissolve the salt in 4 cups water in a large bowl. Pour into a nonreactive saucepan.

2   Rinse the gherkins and add to the brine. Bring the mixture to a boil. Reduce the heat and simmer for 10 minutes.

3   Meanwhile, in another nonreactive saucepan, combine the vinegar, bay leaves, and spices. Warm this mixture, stirring, over low heat for about 5 minutes.

4   Lift the gherkins from the brine using a slotted spoon, rinse, then pack into hot sterilized jars. Pour in the vinegar, ensuring that the spices are evenly divided among the jars and that the gherkins are covered. Add extra vinegar if needed.

5   Seal with vinegar-proof lids, label, and store in a cool, dark place for 1 month before using.

INGREDIENTS

4oz (115g) salt

1lb 2oz (500g) small, firm gherkins (tiny pickling cucumbers)

2 cups white wine vinegar or malt vinegar, plus extra if needed

2 bay leaves

1 tsp white peppercorns

6 cloves

½ tsp allspice berries

1 tsp fennel or dill seeds

Orchard fruit

Cooking apples • Crab apples • Dessert apples
Dried fruits • Figs • Medlars
Pears • Quinces

A rather boozy dessert preserve, spiced pears are a useful pantry standby. Use small pears and make sure you have the fruit completely submerged in the liquid to ensure a good result. Serve with heavy cream, ice cream, or—best of all—chocolate cake and whipped cream.

Pears in white wine with lemongrass

🕐 TAKES 40 MINUTES   🍲 MAKES 12-14 PEARS   🫙 KEEPS FOR 6 MONTHS

1 Cut away 8in (20cm) of the hard root end of the lemongrass and discard. Slice the stem thinly. Using a rolling pin, give the remaining top part of the stalks a good smack, along with the ginger, to release the flavor.

2 In a large nonreactive pot, combine the wine, honey, sugar, sliced and crushed lemongrass, chile, ginger, lime leaves if using, and lemon zest and juice. Bring to a boil and simmer for 5 minutes, stirring until the sugar has dissolved to make a light syrup.

3 Peel the pears, leaving their stems intact. Add the pears to the syrup and poach gently for 20 minutes or until just cooked through. Remove the pears with a slotted spoon and pack into hot sterilized jars.

4 Boil the syrup until thick. Divide among the jars, topping with brandy or vodka, ensuring that the pears are covered. Check weekly, as you may need to add more after a couple of weeks. Seal, label, and store in a cool, dark place for 1 month before using.

INGREDIENTS

4 stalks lemongrass

1in (2.5cm) piece of fresh ginger

1 bottle (750ml) dry white wine

3½oz (100g) honey

1lb (450g) granulated sugar

1 red chile, seeded if desired, and sliced

4–6 kaffir lime leaves, available from Asian stores (optional)

finely grated zest and freshly squeezed juice of 2 lemons

12–14 firm, ripe Bosc or other dessert pears

brandy or vodka, to cover

COOKING AND FLAVORING

These pears become quite soft during cooking, so don't worry about how they will fit into your jars. If you prefer a milder flavor, omit the chile and lemongrass, and use a cinnamon stick and 1 or 2 star anise instead.

Choose firm, ripe pears with a good flavor for this conserve. I like to use Comice or Williams Bon Chrétien. The crystallized ginger adds a surprise element to this unusual recipe.

Pear, apple, and ginger conserve

🕐 TAKES 25 MINUTES   🍲 MAKES 2¾LB (1.25KG)   🗃 KEEPS FOR 6 MONTHS

1 Peel and core the pears and apples, then cut into chunks. Put all the ingredients in a large nonreactive pot, and simmer over medium heat, stirring from time to time, until the sugar has dissolved.

2 Increase the heat and boil the mixture for 15 minutes or until the apples have softened, then test for a set.

3 Once the setting point has been reached, ladle the conserve into hot sterilized jars, seal, and label.

INGREDIENTS

2lb (900g) firm but ripe pears

1¼lb (600g) cooking apples

4oz (115g) crystallized ginger, finely chopped

1lb 5oz (600g) granulated sugar

juice of 2 lemons

grated zest of 1 lemon

Pretty and pink—what more can you ask of a jelly? Crab apples are small enough to be cooked whole, but if there are any bruised or bad spots, simply cut them away.

Crab apple jelly

🕐 TAKES 50 MINUTES   🍲 MAKES 2¼LB (1KG)   🗃 KEEPS FOR 6–9 MONTHS

1 Put the apples and 4 cups water in a large nonreactive pot. Add the lemon rind, ginger, and cinnamon. Bring to a boil, then cover the pan and simmer for 30–40 minutes until the apples have broken down to a pulp. Spoon the mixture into a cheesecloth or other jelly bag and let drip for 6–12 hours.

2 Measure the juice and weigh out the correct amount of sugar. Put the sugar and juice in the cleaned preserving pot, and bring slowly to a boil, stirring until the sugar has dissolved. Cook at a full rolling boil for 5 minutes, then test for a set.

3 When the jelly has reached the setting point, ladle into hot sterilized jars, seal, and label.

INGREDIENTS

3lb 3oz (1.5kg) crab apples

pared rind of 1 lemon

2in (5cm) piece of fresh ginger, peeled and crushed

8in (20cm) cinnamon stick

1lb 2oz (500g) granulated sugar for each 2⅓ cups juice

I'm often asked for a recipe that uses up a lot of apples. This easy preserve can be used in many different ways—spread on buttered toast, stirred into sauces, or served with roasted meats.

Apple butter

⏱ TAKES 3 HOURS   🍲 MAKES 4½LB (2KG)   🥫 KEEPS FOR UP TO I YEAR

1 Put the apples and 15fl oz (450ml) water in a large heavy pan, and simmer for 45–60 minutes until the mixture forms a thick purée.

2 Wrap all the spices loosely in a muslin or cheesecloth bag. Add to the purée with the sugar and stir well. Simmer over very low heat, stirring to dissolve the sugar, for up to 1½ hours. The purée will become very thick and dark in color. If possible, place the pan on a heat diffuser to prevent the mixture from sticking and burning.

3 To test that the butter is ready, allow a spoonful to cool on a plate. When it is ready, it will hold its shape (see p19).

4 Remove the spice bag, ladle into hot sterilized jars, seal, and label.

VARIATION
For a simpler, more subtle flavor, make this apple butter without the spices. Alternatively, you could use the crushed seeds from 6–8 cardamom pods, instead of the cloves.

INGREDIENTS

4lb (1.8kg) peeled, cored, and coarsely chopped cooking apples (prepared weight)

6 cloves, crushed

½ nutmeg, crushed

4in (10cm) cinnamon stick, crushed

2in (5cm) piece of fresh ginger, crushed

3lb (1.35kg) granulated sugar

Preserving with apples

CHOOSING FRUIT

Apples are one of the most useful fruits for making jams and jellies, chutneys, and relishes. They add bulk and can provide pectin, as well as adding acidity to your preserves. To tell if apples are ripe for picking, gently cradle the fruit in your hand and rock it. If the stem separates from the tree, the fruit is ripe. If the apple remains firmly attached, try another day. Use windfalls at once and store hand-picked apples for future use in a cold, dry, dark place.

Types and uses

It is not always necessary to have first rate, unbruised apples. Cut away broken or bruised areas and discard any with insect infestation. Never use an apple that has any trace of mold anywhere, as this might affect the preserve's keeping qualities. Overripe apples and those that have been stored can be used, but their acidity will be low. Apples fall into three groups:

Eating (dessert) apples tend to hold their shape during cooking and include Golden Delicious, Cox's, and Spartan.

Cooking apples break down during cooking and include Bramley, Red Delicious, and Gravenstein.

Crab apples are small and therefore time-consuming to prepare, so are best used for making jelly or added to other jams or jellies to increase yield.

GRAVENSTEIN

COOKING APPLES
These are most often used to add bulk to preserves, but cooking apples are also perfect for making apple butter.

RED DELICIOUS

BRAMLEY

GOLDEN DELICIOUS

SPARTAN

EATING APPLES add both flavor and a chunky texture to preserves, as they hold their shape rather than breaking down into a pulp.

COX'S ORANGE PIPPIN

Easy to produce and so useful to have in the pantry, cinnamon apple jelly can be made from windfall apples or just a bargain buy at the market. Sour cooking apples are best, as dessert apples tend to hold their shape when cooked; in this recipe we're looking for a purée.

Cinnamon apple jelly

🕐 TAKES 70–80 MINUTES   🍲 MAKES 2¾LB (1.25KG)   🥫 KEEPS FOR UP TO 1 YEAR

1   Put the apples and 4 cups water in a large nonreactive pot. Add the lemon rind, ginger, and cinnamon. Bring to a boil, then cover the pan and simmer for 1 hour or until the apples have broken down into a pulp.

2   Spoon the mixture into a cheesecloth or other jelly bag and let drip for 6–12 hours.

3   Measure the juice and weigh out the correct quantity of sugar. Put the sugar and juice in the cleaned preserving pot, and bring the mixture slowly to a boil, stirring until the sugar has dissolved. Increase the heat and cook at a full rolling boil for 10 minutes, then test for a set.

4   When the jelly has reached the setting point, remove any scum from the surface with a slotted spoon. Ladle the jelly into hot sterilized jars. (You can put a piece of cinnamon stick in each jar before adding the jelly, if desired.) Seal and label.

VARIATION
Orange rind and cloves can replace the lemon rind and cinnamon here. The rich flavor they add is particularly good with hot buttered toast.

INGREDIENTS

3lb 3oz (1.5kg) cooking apples, diced

thinly pared rind of 1 lemon

2in (5cm) piece of fresh ginger, peeled and crushed

8in (20cm) cinnamon stick, roughly broken, plus extra if desired (see method)

1lb 2oz (500g) granulated sugar for each 2⅓ cups juice

Medlars are an acquired taste. Hard when harvested, they need to be kept in a dark place for 6–8 weeks to soften until almost rotten. If you have a medlar tree in your garden, they produce fruit prolifically. This jelly makes the best use of them. Serve with game, meat pies, and terrines.

Medlar jelly

TAKES 60 MINUTES   MAKES 3LB 3OZ (1.5KG)   KEEPS FOR UP TO 1 YEAR

1   Put the medlars and 4 cups water in a large nonreactive pot, and simmer for 30–40 minutes until the fruit is very soft.

2   Spoon the mixture into a cheesecloth or other jelly bag and allow to drip overnight.

3   Measure the juice: you will have approximately 4 cups. Weigh out the appropriate amount of sugar. Pour the juice into the cleaned nonreactive pot, and add the sugar and lemon juice.

4   Bring the mixture slowly to a boil, stirring often, until the sugar has dissolved. Cook at a full rolling boil for 2–3 minutes.

5   Add the pectin. Return the mixture to a boil and cook for another minute before testing for a set.

6   When the jelly has reached the setting point, ladle into hot sterilized jars, seal, and label.

VARIATION
While it is true that medlars have a pronounced flavor all their own, adding a 4in (10cm) piece of fresh ginger, peeled and finely grated, at the same time as you add the sugar, works well in this recipe.

INGREDIENTS

4½lb (2kg) medlars

freshly squeezed juice of 3 lemons

4½oz (125g) liquid pectin

3oz (85g) granulated sugar for each 3½fl oz (100ml) juice

This recipe comes from the traditional cuisine of the Western Cape region of South Africa and makes wonderful use of green—that is, unripe—figs. When cooked, the fruits turn a deep, translucent bottle-green. Serve with thinly sliced, buttered white bread, or with desserts.

Green fig preserve

⏱ TAKES UP TO 2¼ HOURS   🍲 MAKES 2¼LB (1KG)   🫙 KEEPS FOR 6 MONTHS

1 In a large glass or china bowl, dissolve the salt in 8 cups water to make the brine.

2 Cut a small cross in the base of each fig and scrape the skins if they are very fuzzy. Put the prepared figs in the brine, and let sit for 24 hours.

3 Drain the figs and rinse under cold running water. Put in a nonreactive saucepan, cover with water, and add the baking soda. Bring to a boil and simmer for 10–15 minutes until the figs are just tender. Drain.

4 Meanwhile, make the syrup. Put the sugar and 1¼ cups water in a nonreactive pot and bring to a boil. Add the ginger. Simmer for about 5 minutes until the syrup thickens slightly.

5 Lift the figs into the syrup, and simmer gently over low heat for 1–2 hours until the figs are translucent.

6 Drain the figs, reserving the syrup. Pack into hot sterilized jars and cover with the syrup, discarding the ginger. Seal and label.

VARIATION
To give this preserve an extra kick, add a few mild fresh green chiles, seeded and sliced, at the same time as you add the ginger.

INGREDIENTS

3½oz (100g) salt

2¼lb (1kg) unripe green figs, stems intact

1 tsp baking soda

FOR THE SYRUP

2¼lb (1kg) granulated sugar

4in (10cm) piece of fresh ginger, lightly crushed

Fig trees are often prolific producers. As the fruits all seem to ripen at once and must be saved from the ravages of wasps, preserving is an excellent alternative to overindulgence. I have a Brown Turkey tree and use those for my jam, but other varieties also work well. As well as the obvious uses, fig jam works well with cheeses, especially toasted goat cheese and pecorino.

Fig jam

🕐 TAKES 45 MINUTES　　🍲 MAKES 3LB (1.35KG)　　🫙 KEEPS FOR 6 MONTHS

1　Cut the hard stems from the tops of the figs and peel. Cut the flesh into ½in (1cm) chunks.

2　Put the figs, lemon juice, and zest in a large nonreactive pot. Simmer over low heat for about 30 minutes until the figs are very soft.

3　Add the sugar and continue to simmer over low heat, stirring, until the sugar has dissolved.

4　Stir in the pectin, increase the heat, and cook at a full rolling boil for 10 minutes, then test for a set.

5　When the jam has reached the setting point, ladle into hot sterilized jars, seal, and label.

INGREDIENTS

2½lb (1.1kg) ripe figs

freshly squeezed juice of 2 lemons

finely grated zest of 1 lemon

2¼lb (1kg) granulated sugar

4½oz (125g) liquid pectin

RETAINING THE SEEDS

Like raspberry jam, fig jam contains a large number of seeds. I think this is an important part of its character and so prefer not to sieve these out. If your preference is for a smooth preserve, however, you could rub the mixture through a fine sieve once the sugar has dissolved, but before you add the pectin.

Quince trees take several years to mature, but once they begin to produce fruit, you are assured of the essential ingredient for this delicious preserve, also known as membrillo. *My recipe has been adapted from* The Boston Cooking School Cookbook *published in the 19th century.*

Quince cheese

⏱ TAKES UP TO 3 HOURS   🥘 MAKES 2¾LB (1.25KG)   🫙 KEEPS FOR UP TO 3 YEARS

1 Cut the quinces into chunks about 1¾in (4cm) in size. Put in a saucepan and cover with water. Simmer for 30 minutes, partially covered, until the quinces are very soft. You may need to add more water. Alternatively, wrap the quinces in foil and bake in a 350°F (180°C) oven for about 1 hour until they are soft.

2 Mash the fruit coarsely, and rub through a fine sieve to produce a smooth purée.

3 Put the purée in a heavy nonreactive pot with the sugar and lemon juice. Simmer over low heat for 20 minutes, stirring frequently, until the sugar has dissolved.

4 Increase the heat to medium and simmer, stirring frequently, until the purée is very thick. It will darken slightly. Watch carefully as this preserve can scorch and burn.

5 Ladle the cheese into hot sterilized jars, seal, and label.

INGREDIENTS

2¼lb (1kg) quinces

2lb (900g) granulated sugar

freshly squeezed juice of 3 lemons

CHOOSING FRUIT

I try to find the largest quinces around for this preserve, as they cook much more quickly than the small, hard ones found on my bushes. Don't worry about any small blemishes on the fruit—just cut them away.

This is a real autumn relish—the plums add both sharpness and rich seasonal color. Relying on fresh spices rather than dried ones, this preserve has a light, refreshing flavor. It goes especially well with cold meats, grilled pork chops, or mature cheeses.

Apple, plum, and onion relish

🕐 TAKES 60 MINUTES　　🥘 MAKES 3½LB (1.6KG)　　🫙 KEEPS FOR UP TO 1 YEAR

1　In the bowl of a small food processor or a mortar and pestle, process the garlic, ginger, and chiles into a paste.

2　Put all the ingredients except the sage in a nonreactive pot, and bring to a boil, stirring, until the sugar has dissolved.

3　Over a medium-low heat, simmer the relish for 40 minutes or until it is reduced and thick. Stir in the sage and continue to simmer for another 2–3 minutes until it has reached the desired consistency.

4　Ladle the relish into hot sterilized jars, cover with vinegar-proof seals, and label. Store in a cool, dark place.

VARIATION

While I have chosen to use red plums here, a glut of yellow plums would be a perfect alternative for this relish.

INGREDIENTS

5 plump garlic cloves

4in (10cm) piece of fresh ginger, peeled and chopped

2 green chiles, seeded if desired, and chopped

2¼lb (1kg) cooking apples, peeled, cored, and chopped

1½lb (675g) sweet onions, peeled and chopped

1lb 2oz (500g) red plums, stoned and chopped

1½ cups cider vinegar

10oz (300g) granulated sugar

1 tbsp salt

2 tbsp chopped fresh sage

Using two different types of apples produces the characteristic chunkiness of this classic sauce.

Chunky apple sauce

🕐 TAKES 30 MINUTES　　🥣 MAKES 3½LB (1.6KG)　　🗄 KEEPS FOR 3 MONTHS

1　Peel, core, and coarsely chop the cooking apples. Put in a large nonreactive pot with 14fl oz (400ml) water and simmer for 10 minutes, or until the apples soften and break down to a purée.

2　Meanwhile, peel, core, and cut the dessert apples into 1½in (1cm) dice. Add to the cooking apples with the sugar and lemon juice. Bring the mixture to a boil, and simmer for 20 minutes until there is little excess liquid and the sauce is thick.

3　Ladle into hot sterilized jars, seal, label, and store in a cool, dark place.

INGREDIENTS

2¼lb (1kg) cooking apples

4 firm dessert apples

10oz (300g) granulated sugar

freshly squeezed juice of 2 lemons

This is a wonderfully useful chutney, made from orchard fruit and the last of the tomatoes.

Pear, apple, and tomato chutney

🕐 TAKES 80 MINUTES　　🥣 MAKES 5½LB (2.5KG)　　🗄 KEEPS FOR UP TO 1 YEAR

1　To skin the tomatoes, cut a cross in the base of each one and immerse for 1–2 minutes in a bowl of boiling water. When the skins start to loosen, drain the tomatoes, peel, and chop the flesh. Chop the onions. Peel, core, and chop the apples and pears. Crush the garlic, and grate the ginger. Seed the chiles if desired, and chop.

2　Put all the ingredients in a nonreactive pot, and bring slowly to a boil, stirring until the sugar has dissolved. Increase the heat to medium, and simmer the chutney for 1¼ hours or until thick.

3　Ladle into hot sterilized jars, cover with vinegar-proof seals, and label.

INGREDIENTS

1½lb (675g) ripe tomatoes

1lb (450g) onions

2¾lb (1.25kg) cooking apples

1lb 2oz (500g) firm pears

4–6 garlic cloves

3½oz (100g) fresh ginger

1–2 red chiles

1lb (450g) raisins

1 tbsp salt

3¾ cups white wine vinegar

1lb 10oz (750g) Demerara or raw sugar

This lovely recipe comes from my mother and is a good way to use up a windfall crop of apples.

Easy apple and onion chutney

🕒 TAKES 60 MINUTES   🍲 MAKES 8LB (3.6KG)   🫙 KEEPS FOR UP TO 1 YEAR

1 Peel, core, and chop the apples. Chop the onions, garlic, and ginger. Seed the chile if desired, and chop. Put the apples, onions, garlic, ginger, and chile in a large nonreactive pot. Pour in the vinegar and stir in the sugar, turmeric, and salt.

2 Bring the mixture to a boil, stirring until the sugar has dissolved, then simmer for about 1 hour until thick. Stir often as the mixture reduces, to avoid it sticking to the bottom of the pan and burning.

3 Spoon into hot sterilized jars, cover with vinegar-proof seals, label, and store in a cool, dark place for about 1 month before using.

INGREDIENTS

4lb (1.8kg) cooking apples

2lb (900g) onions

3–4 plump garlic cloves

2oz (60g) fresh ginger

1 large red chile

4 cups distilled malt vinegar

1¼lb (550g) light brown or muscovado sugar

2 tbsp ground turmeric

1 tbsp salt

Relatively smooth, this tasty, tangy chutney is perfect for cheese and cold meat sandwiches.

Curried apple and date chutney

🕒 TAKES 80 MINUTES   🍲 MAKES 10LB (4.5KG)   🫙 KEEPS FOR UP TO 1 YEAR

1 Peel, core, and quarter the apples. Chop the onions, dates, ginger, and garlic. Put all the ingredients except the sugar in a large nonreactive pot and simmer for 20 minutes over medium heat until the apples have begun to soften. Add the sugar and simmer for another 5 minutes, stirring occasionally, until the sugar has dissolved.

2 Increase the heat and boil the chutney for 45–50 minutes, stirring often, until well reduced and thick.

3 Ladle into hot sterilized jars, cover with vinegar-proof seals, and label.

INGREDIENTS

4½lb (2kg) cooking apples

6 large onions

1lb 2oz (500g) pitted dates

4in (10cm) piece fresh ginger

4–8 plump garlic cloves

2 tbsp salt

4 cups malt vinegar

2–3 tbsp Madras curry paste

2¼lb (1kg) light brown or muscovado sugar

Choose whatever combination of dried fruit suits your taste—such as apricots, figs, peaches, and raisins—but try to make it as varied as possible. The chutney takes very little time to cook, as the high proportion of dried fruit helps it thicken quickly.

Dried fruit and apple chutney

🕐 TAKES UP TO 1 HOUR   🍲 MAKES 1KG (2¼LB)   📦 KEEPS FOR UP TO 1 YEAR

1   Cut the larger dried fruits into even-sized pieces, about ½in (1cm) in size.

2   Put the dried fruit, apples, onions, garlic, ginger, chiles, sugar, and salt in a large heavy nonreactive pot. Add the vinegar and stir so that all the ingredients are well combined.

3   Bring the mixture to a boil, reduce the heat, and simmer for 30–45 minutes, stirring occasionally, until the mixture has reached the desired consistency.

4   Ladle into hot sterilized jars, cover with vinegar-proof seals, and label. Store in a cool, dark place.

VARIATION
Apples add the bulk and fresh flavor here, but any other fruit, if found in plentiful supply, can be used instead, such as pears, plums, or mangoes.

INGREDIENTS

1½lb (675g) mixed dried fruit

3lb (1.35kg) cooking apples, peeled and chopped

2 large onions, chopped

6 plump garlic cloves, chopped

2in (5cm) piece of fresh ginger, grated

1–2 dried red chiles, crushed

1½lb (675g) light brown or muscovado sugar

1 tbsp salt

4 cups cider or distilled malt vinegar

Flowers and herbs

Elderflowers • Geraniums • Lavender • Lemon verbena
Mint • Nasturtiums • Rosemary • Roses • Sage
Tarragon • Thyme

Pink rose petals suspended in clear pink, wine-flavored jelly, fragranced with rose water, make this one of the prettiest and most unusual of all preserves. Rose waters differ in strength; try to find a full-bodied one for this recipe. This jelly is delicious with scones for afternoon tea, or served with breakfast in bed on Valentine's Day.

Rosé wine and rose petal jelly

🕐 TAKES 20 MINUTES   🍲 MAKES 2¾LB (1.25KG)   🥫 KEEPS FOR 9–12 MONTHS

1   In a heavy nonreactive pot, combine the wine with the sugar. Stir the mixture over low heat until the sugar has completely dissolved. Increase the heat and bring the mixture to a full rolling boil. Boil for 2 minutes, skimming off any scum that rises to the surface.

2   Remove from the heat and stir in the pectin. Return the mixture to the heat and bring back to a boil. Boil for 1 minute, then stir in the rose water.

3   Add the rose petals and ladle the jelly into hot sterilized jars. Place the lids lightly on top, and allow the jelly to set for about 15 minutes.

4   Using a sterilized metal spoon, gently stir the petals down into the setting jelly.

5   Once the jelly has set, tighten the lids and label the jars.

INGREDIENTS

3 cups rosé wine

1¾lb (800g) granulated sugar

6oz (175g) liquid pectin

¼ cup rose water

2 handfuls of unsprayed rose petals

CHOOSING AND PICKING PETALS

Small rose petals work well in this recipe. They should be freshly picked, dry, and unblemished. Match the petals to the color of the wine. Pale pink ones will best be complemented by a delicately colored rosé, while for a richer, more jewel-like hue, try a Shiraz rosé with petals from a deep red rose.

Flavored with scented geranium leaves, this jelly is evocative of summer days in the garden. Rose-scented leaves are especially good. For extra tanginess, add the juice of 2 lemons.

Scented geranium leaf jelly

🕐 TAKES 50 MINUTES   🍲 MAKES 2¾LB (1.25KG)   🫙 KEEPS FOR 6–9 MONTHS

1 Put the apples and 4 cups water in a large nonreactive pot. Add the geranium leaves and bring to a boil. Cover and simmer for 40 minutes, or until the apples have broken down to a pulp. Spoon the mixture into a cheesecloth or other jelly bag and let drip for 6–12 hours.

2 Measure the resulting liquid and weigh out the correct quantity of sugar. Put the sugar and juice in the cleaned preserving pot. Bring slowly to a boil, stirring until the sugar has dissolved. Increase the heat and cook at a full rolling boil for 10 minutes, then test for a set.

3 When the jelly has reached the setting point, ladle into hot sterilized jars, placing a couple of small leaves on top of the jelly. Seal and label.

INGREDIENTS

3lb 3oz (1.5kg) cooking apples

12 unsprayed scented geranium leaves, plus extra for garnish

1lb 2oz (500g) granulated sugar for each 2⅓ cups juice

This sophisticated crystal-clear jelly is as simple to make as it is delicious. Serve with cold meats, pork roasts, and with roast duck or goose.

Sage and sauternes jelly

🕐 TAKES 10 MINUTES   🍲 MAKES 2¾LB (1.25KG)   🫙 KEEPS FOR 6–9 MONTHS

1 In a heavy nonreactive pot, combine the wine and sugar, and stir over low heat until the sugar has dissolved. Increase the heat and bring the mixture to a full rolling boil, and boil for 2 minutes.

2 Turn off the heat and stir in the pectin. Bring the mixture back to a boil and boil for 1 minute, then test for a set.

3 Once the jelly has reached the setting point, add the leaves and flowers, if using, and allow to settle for 10 minutes before ladling into hot sterilized jars. Let stand for another 15 minutes, covered, stirring the herbs down into the jelly with a sterilized metal spoon if necessary. Seal and label.

INGREDIENTS

3 cups Sauternes or other sweet white wine

1¾lb (800g) granulated sugar

9oz (250g) liquid pectin

handful of small fresh unsprayed sage leaves, thinly sliced

1 tbsp unsprayed sage flowers (optional)

This adaptable herb jelly is perfect with roast lamb, and is also delicious on toast. Using apples as a base, it is scented with both rosemary stems and flowers.

Rosemary jelly

🕐 TAKES 50 MINUTES   🍲 MAKES 3LB (1.35KG)   📦 KEEPS FOR 6–9 MONTHS

1 Put the apples and 4 cups water in a large nonreactive pot and add the rosemary sprigs. Bring the mixture to a boil, cover the pan, and simmer for 40 minutes or until the apples have broken down into a pulp.

2 Spoon the mixture into a cheesecloth or other jelly bag, and let drip for at least 6 hours or preferably overnight.

3 Measure the juice and weigh out the correct quantity of sugar. Put both in the cleaned preserving pot and bring to a boil, stirring frequently, until the sugar has dissolved.

4 Once the sugar has dissolved, increase the heat and cook the jelly at a full rolling boil for 5–10 minutes, skimming off any scum that rises to the surface, then test for a set.

5 When the jelly has reached the setting point, add the rosemary flowers, if using, and simmer for another 30 seconds.

6 Allow the jelly to cool for about 5 minutes, before stirring gently with a sterilized metal spoon to distribute the flowers. Ladle into hot sterilized jars, seal, and label.

VARIATION
Other herbs can be used here in place of the rosemary: sage, thyme, and marjoram all work well.

INGREDIENTS

3lb 3oz (1.5kg) cooking apples, peeled, cored, and diced

6–8 sprigs of fresh unsprayed rosemary, coarsely chopped

1lb 2oz (500g) granulated sugar for each 2⅓ cups juice

handful of unsprayed rosemary flowers (optional)

Few herbs are more evocative of the scented summer garden than lavender. Here, it adds its fragrance to a pretty jelly, just right for an elegant tea. Blackberries provide color; if you want a more jewel-like hue, use a few drops of red food coloring as well.

Lavender jelly

🕐 TAKES UP TO 1 HOUR   🍲 MAKES 3LB 3OZ (1.5KG)   🗄 KEEPS FOR 6–9 MONTHS

1 Put the apples, blackberries, 2 tablespoons of the lavender flowers, and 6 cups water in a large nonreactive pot. Simmer for 40–50 minutes until the apples are very soft.

2 Put the pulp in a cheesecloth or other jelly bag and let drip for several hours. Don't be tempted to squeeze the bag, as the jelly will be clouded if you do.

3 Measure the resulting juice and weigh out the correct quantity of sugar. Put the juice, sugar, a few drops of food coloring, if using, and the remaining flowers in the cleaned nonreactive pot. Bring slowly to a boil. Cook at a full rolling boil for 5 minutes, skimming off any scum that rises to the surface, then test for a set.

4 Once the jelly has reached the setting point, ladle into hot sterilized jars, seal, and label.

INGREDIENTS

4lb (1.8kg) cooking apples, cored and diced

a few blackberries, for color

3 tbsp unsprayed lavender flowers

1lb (450g) granulated sugar for each 2⅓ cups juice

red food coloring (optional)

CHECKING THE FLOWERS

Always check flowers before you use them to see that they are not harboring any insects, and smell the flowers, too—the flavor is scent-related, so a dull scent equals a dull preserve. Most importantly, remember to ensure that the flowers are actually edible, and avoid any flowers that have been sprayed with pesticides.

Preserving with flowers and herbs

PICKING AND PREPARING

Using flowers and herbs to flavor and season preserves links us with the apothecaries and herbalists of history. Gather your flowers and herbs early on a dry day. Flowers should be just at the point of full bloom before any wilting begins. With larger blooms, check for insect activity and gently tap the flowers to dislodge unwanted inhabitants. If your herbs and flowers are clean, dust-free, and growing out of range of pet activity, there is no need to wash them—although you must be very sure they have not been sprayed with any pesticides. If they are gritty, or a pesticide suitable for use on edible crops has been used, you must rinse them thoroughly. Lay on clean dry dish towels to dry fully before use.

BAY LEAVES are useful for flavoring sugars, vinegars, and other savory preserves.

ROSE PETALS, from buds on the point of opening, are best for jellies and sugars. Choose varieties with small petals and use soon after picking.

LAVENDER is most heady when the florets are deeply colored and not quite open. Dry on a clean dish towel in the sun for 2–3 days if not using at once.

ROSEMARY is a strongly scented herb. Use the soft, small shoots, and try to include some of the flowers—they taste delicious.

MINT comes in many varieties. Choose the small, newer leaves and remove all the coarse stems before chopping. Use at once.

LEMONGRASS is a popular flavoring in Southeast Asian cuisine. The pale green stalks can be used to impart a lemony tang to preserves.

GERANIUM and other scented leaves, such as lemon verbena and black currant, can add flavor to vinegars and sugars to good effect.

THYME has a distinctive flavor and should be picked and used in the same way as rosemary.

BASIL should, if possible, be the small-leaved Greek type, as it has an intense scent without too much water in the leaves.

SAGE can add flavor to jellies and sugars. Use the soft end shoots, and flowers if available.

A traditional accompaniment to lamb, this jelly is easy to make and stores well. You can add a few drops of green food coloring to the jelly if you like, but I prefer to leave it natural.

Mint jelly

🕐 TAKES 20 MINUTES   🥘 MAKES 1KG (2¼LB)   🍯 KEEPS FOR 6 MONTHS

1 Using a food processor finely chop the lemon shells. Put in a heavy saucepan with 3 cups water, and bring to a boil. Simmer for 15 minutes, then let drip through a cheesecloth or other jelly bag for 2 hours.

2 Measure the liquid and add water, if needed, to make it up to 2 cups. Pour this into a nonreactive pot, and add the sugar and vinegar. Stir over low heat until the sugar has dissolved.

3 Increase the heat and cook at a full rolling boil for 3 minutes, then test for a set.

4 When the jelly has reached the setting point, stir in the mint. Ladle the jelly into hot sterilized jars, cover with vinegar-proof seals, and label.

INGREDIENTS

shells from 4 lemons (see p208)

1lb (2oz 500g) sugar

6 tbsp white wine vinegar

2 good handfuls of fresh mint, finely chopped

You may already have a jar of vanilla sugar on the shelf, but why not prolong the sweetness of summer by making aromatic sugars with herbs and flowers? Lavender is my favorite. Lemon verbena, rose, thyme, and rosemary also work well, but I find the flavor of sage a bit antiseptic.

Sweet herb sugars

🕐 NO COOKING   🥘 MAKES 9OZ (250G)   🍯 KEEPS FOR UP TO 1 YEAR

1 Fill one-third of a sterilized jar with sugar, and sprinkle with some of the herbs or flowers. Build alternate layers in this manner until the jar is full. Repeat with any other jars.

2 Seal, label, and let stand to infuse for at least 1 week before using. If desired, you can sieve the sugar before using to remove the herbs or flowers, but in my recipes, I prefer to leave the sugar unsieved.

INGREDIENTS

9oz (250g) superfine sugar

a good handful of unsprayed herbs or flowers, such as lavender flowers, rosemary leaves or flowers, thyme leaves, or lemon verbena leaves

Green tea has wonderful antioxidant properties. Whether they are present in this jelly I can't say, but I like to think that something that is both fragrant and delicious must be good for you.

Green tea and lime jelly

⏱ TAKES 10 MINUTES　　🍲 MAKES 2¼LB (1KG)　　🥫 KEEPS FOR 6 MONTHS

1　Put the tea leaves, lime zest, and a few jasmine flowers in a large heatproof glass bowl. Pour in 4 cups boiling water and let sit to infuse for 1–2 hours.

2　Strain the tea into a nonreactive saucepan, and add the lime juice and sugar. Stir over low heat until the sugar has dissolved, then add the pectin, stirring well.

3　Increase the heat and bring the mixture to a boil. Cook at a full rolling boil for 2–3 minutes, skimming off any scum that rises to the surface, then test for a set.

4　When the jelly has reached the setting point, stir in the extra jasmine flowers. Let cool for about 10 minutes, then ladle the jelly into hot sterilized jars, seal, and label.

VARIATION

Edible jasmine flowers are available from some Asian markets as well as specialist suppliers that also sell green teas, rosebuds, etc. If you cannot find any, omit the jasmine flowers and use 2 tablespoons loose jasmine tea leaves, or a green tea and jasmine mix, instead.

INGREDIENTS

1–2 tbsp green tea leaves

finely grated zest of 3 limes

a few unsprayed jasmine flowers, plus extra to decorate

freshly squeezed juice of 2 large limes

1lb 10oz (750g) granulated sugar

4½oz (125g) liquid pectin

Herb vinegars are a wonderful addition to the cook's repertoire of flavors. I like to scent vinegar with tarragon, a soft herb that does not dry well. Pick it early in the morning on a dry day when it will be fullest in flavor and when insect activity is at its lowest. Use good-quality vinegar: both white wine and cider vinegars are excellent.

Tarragon vinegar

🕐 NO COOKING   🍲 MAKES 1½ CUPS   🗄 KEEPS FOR 1 YEAR

1 Put the tarragon in a glass bowl with the vinegar. Cover the bowl tightly with two layers of plastic wrap, and let sit for 7 days to infuse in a cool, dark place.

2 Strain the vinegar, then pour it into a sterilized bottle. Push in a couple of sprigs of the freshly picked tarragon, and close the bottle with a vinegar-proof seal.

3 Store the vinegar in a cool, dark place.

VARIATION

This simple recipe can be adapted for use with other herbs, according to preference and availability. Try making it with fresh chervil or basil instead of tarragon. A selection of herb vinegars on your shelves will be a good pantry standby.

INGREDIENTS

a good handful of dry fresh tarragon, coarsely chopped, plus extra freshly picked, unsprayed tarragon sprigs

1½ cups white wine vinegar or cider vinegar

This wonderfully fragrant cordial is so easy to make and so delicious in summer drinks, fruit salads, sorbets, and jellies. Pick elderflowers first thing in the morning, shaking gently to remove any wildlife. To minimize the risk of the cordial fermenting, it is essential that you use spotlessly clean utensils. Citric acid is available from Asian, Polish, and Jewish grocery stores.

Elderflower cordial

🕐 TAKES 5 MINUTES   🥘 MAKES 6 CUPS   🥫 KEEPS FOR 6 MONTHS

1 Put the sugar and 6 cups water in a large saucepan, and boil for 5 minutes, stirring occasionally, to dissolve the sugar.

2 Chop the lemons, oranges, and limes into 1in (2.5cm) cubes. Put in a large, spotlessly clean heatproof glass or china bowl with the dry flowerheads. Pour in the hot syrup, stir in the citric acid, and cover with a clean cloth. Leave the bowl in a cool, dark place for 4 days, stirring each day with a clean spoon.

3 Strain the syrup through scalded muslin or cheesecloth, and pour into sterilized bottles. Seal and label. Store in the refrigerator. To serve, dilute the cordial with water to taste.

VARIATION

For a more tart, refreshing drink, replace one of the oranges with two extra limes—perfect for cooling you down on a hot summer's day.

INGREDIENTS

2¼lb (1kg) granulated sugar

2 organic or unwaxed lemons

2 organic or unwaxed oranges

4 organic or unwaxed limes

about 20 large elderflower heads (see p152)

2oz (60g) citric acid

Pretty in the garden, nasturtiums are also useful in the kitchen. The flowers are both delicious and attractive in salads, and the seed pods can be pickled and used like capers. However, the plants are rather prone to blackfly. If you need to spray them, make sure you use a spray that is not harmful when eaten. Pick young berries before the pods turn yellow and the seeds harden.

Pickled nasturtium berries

🕐 NO COOKING   🥘 MAKES 14OZ (400G)   🥫 KEEPS FOR 6 MONTHS

1 To make the brine, combine the salt and 2 cups water in a large glass or china bowl, stirring until the salt has dissolved.

2 Add the berries and let sit for 24 hours, then drain well and set aside.

3 In a nonreactive saucepan, combine the vinegar, bay leaves, dill, and peppercorns, and bring to a boil. Once the vinegar is boiling, turn off the heat.

4 Pack the nasturtium berries into a hot sterilized jar, and pour in the hot herb vinegar. Seal with a vinegar-proof lid, and store in a cool, dark place. Let sit for 4 weeks before using.

VARIATION

A few green peppercorns sprinkled into the vinegar with the white peppercorns add a lovely flavor to this unusual pickle.

INGREDIENTS

1¾oz (50g) salt

1 teacup of nasturtium berries with short stems

1 cup white wine vinegar

2 bay leaves

a few sprigs of fresh dill

½ tsp white peppercorns, lightly crushed

Wild harvest

Blackberries • Chestnuts • Cloudberries • Elderberries
Juniper berries • Rosehips • Rowan berries • Horseradish
Samphire • Sloes • Walnuts

This is one of the easiest jams to make and a great favorite with my mother-in-law, Nancy Prince, who had an orchard and a few blackberry bushes. Apples are rich in pectin and acid, while blackberries add color and extra flavor. This jam is delicious spooned over rich Greek-style yogurt.

Blackberry and apple jam

🕐 TAKES 40 MINUTES　🍲 MAKES 2¾LB (1.25KG)　🫙 KEEPS FOR UP TO 1 YEAR

1　Put the apples and blackberries in a heavy nonreactive pot with the lemon juice, 7fl oz (200ml) water, and the sugar. Simmer over low heat for about 30 minutes until the sugar has dissolved, and the apples have broken down to a pulp. Mash with a wooden spoon.

2　Increase the heat and cook the mixture at a full rolling boil for 10 minutes, then test for a set. Using a slotted spoon, skim off any scum that has formed on the surface of the jam.

3　Once the jam has reached the setting point, ladle into hot sterilized jars, seal, and label.

INGREDIENTS

2¼lb (1kg) cooking apples, peeled, cored, and chopped

10oz (300g) blackberries

freshly squeezed juice of 1 lemon

2¼lb (1kg) granulated sugar

MAKING THE MOST OF WINDFALLS

This recipe produces a beautiful jewel-colored firm preserve. As this is essentially a jam made from windfall apples and wild berries, you do not need to worry if the apples are bruised—simply cut away any blemishes. The final result will still be delicious.

Ripe elderberries and blackberries may be gathered in late summer or early autumn. Don't forget to wash the fruit in warm water to make sure that it has no dust or animal residue on it.

Wild berry jam

🕐 TAKES 40 MINUTES　　🍲 MAKES 3½LB (1.6KG)　　🥫 KEEPS FOR 6–9 MONTHS

1　Put the plums in a bowl with 9oz (250g) sugar, and let stand for 2–4 hours to draw out the juice.

2　Put the berries and 3½fl oz (100ml) water in a nonreactive pot, and simmer for 15–20 minutes until the fruit is soft. For a smoother jam, press through a coarse sieve. Return to the pot. Add the plums, the remaining sugar, the vinegar, and the lemon juice.

3　Simmer over low heat until the sugar has dissolved. Increase the heat and cook the mixture at a full rolling boil for 10–15 minutes, then test for a set.

4　Once the jam has reached the setting point, ladle into hot sterilized jars, seal, and label.

INGREDIENTS

2¼lb (1kg) purple plums, pitted and coarsely chopped

3lb (1.35kg) granulated sugar

2¼lb (1kg) mixed elderberries and blackberries

1 tbsp cider vinegar

freshly squeezed juice of 1 lemon

These beautiful berries confuse the novice picker because they are red when unripe and golden when ripe. They grow in the Northern Hemisphere and have a raspberry-like flavor.

Cloudberry jam

🕐 TAKES 20 MINUTES　　🍲 MAKES 1LB 5OZ (600G)　　🥫 KEEPS FOR 6 MONTHS

1　Put the berries in a heavy nonreactive pot, with just the water that remains on them after rinsing. Heat slowly until the berries soften, then boil for 5 minutes. Add the sugar and continue to cook, stirring, until the sugar has dissolved.

2　Stir in the pectin and lemon juice. Increase the heat and cook at a full rolling boil for 2 minutes, then test for a set.

3　Once the jam has reached the setting point, ladle into hot sterilized jars, seal, and label.

INGREDIENTS

1lb 2oz (500g) cloudberries, hulled and washed

11oz (325g) granulated sugar

4½oz (125g) liquid pectin

freshly squeezed juice of 1 lemon

Brambles are the cultivated blackberry's wild cousins. Picking the berries may result in thorn-scratched arms and fingers, but this delicious jelly more than makes up for the experience.

Bramble jelly

🕐 TAKES 30 MINUTES   🍲 MAKES 2¾LB (1.25KG)   🫙 KEEPS FOR 9 MONTHS

1　Put the berries, apples, and 2 cups water in a nonreactive pot. Simmer the mixture for 10 minutes, then spoon into a cheesecloth or other jelly bag and let drip overnight.

2　Measure the juice and weigh out the correct quantity of sugar. Pour the juice into the cleaned pot and add the sugar. Cook over medium heat, stirring, until the sugar has dissolved.

3　Increase the heat and cook at a full rolling boil for 3 minutes, then test for a set.

4　Once the jelly has reached the setting point, ladle into hot sterilized jars, seal, and label.

INGREDIENTS

2¼lb (1kg) wild blackberries, rinsed

2 large cooking apples, chopped

3½oz (100g) granulated sugar for each 3½fl oz (100ml) juice

This pretty pink jelly is delicious with hot buttered toast or biscuits. Resist the temptation to squeeze the bag as the juice drips, or the resulting jelly will be cloudy.

Rose hip jelly

🕐 TAKES 50 MINUTES   🍲 MAKES 2¼LB (1KG)   🫙 KEEPS FOR 6 MONTHS

1　Rinse the rose hips and remove the stems. Put in a nonreactive pot with 4 cups water, and simmer for 40 minutes, or until the rose hips are soft. Transfer to a jelly bag and let drip for 12 hours.

2　Measure the juice: you should have about 3¾ cups. Put in a nonreactive pot with the sugar, lemon juice, and pectin. Bring the mixture slowly to a boil, stirring to dissolve the sugar, then cook at a full rolling boil for 2 minutes. Test for a set.

3　Once the jelly has reached the setting point, ladle into hot sterilized jars, seal, and label.

INGREDIENTS

2¼lb (1kg) rose hips

1lb 10oz (750g) granulated sugar

freshly squeezed juice of 2–3 lemons, about ½ cup

9oz (250g) liquid pectin

Foraging for wild food

BEFORE YOU BEGIN

When setting off on a walk with foraging in mind, the first question you must ask yourself is: "Am I legally allowed to forage for food here?" It is essential that you make sure you are not trespassing or taking away plants that are protected on otherwise open land. Don't be greedy—just take your share and leave the rest for others, and for the plants themselves to regenerate.

Choosing and picking

You will need a knife, brown paper bags, baskets for fruit, and appropriate clothing made of sturdy material for tackling bramble bushes and protecting you from other prickly plants. A good pair of gardening gloves is also handy.

Elderflowers (see p144) are at their best picked in the early morning before the insects get busy. Choose young blooms with a heady fragrance.

Wild berries such as rowan berries and blackberries should be gathered on dry days and picked from only those boughs above dog level.

Horseradish needs to be dug up, so a small fork is useful. Leave some of the root so that the plant can continue to grow.

Samphire (Salicornia) should be picked when small, and pulled directly from the mud.

Nuts should be within easy reach—otherwise you must wait until the nuts fall.

ROSE HIPS High in vitamin C and iron, the plump red hips from the dog rose, Rosa Canina, are found in abundance from midsummer.

ROWAN BERRIES Often used by herbalists, Rowan berries have a high content of both vitamins A and C. They make wonderful jellies.

BLACKBERRIES Cousin of the domestic cultivar, wild blackberries have an intense flavor, and they should be gathered early in the autumn before the fruit withers.

Packed with vitamin C, rose hip syrup makes a delightful cordial. Gather fully ripe red hips from rosebushes. You can tell if they are ready for picking by squeezing them gently: they should give slightly to the touch. Rose hip syrup is delicious spooned over creamy desserts, such as vanilla ice cream, or diluted with water as a late summer drink.

Rose hip syrup

🕐 TAKES 60–80 MINUTES   🍲 MAKES 4 CUPS   🗄 KEEPS FOR 6 MONTHS

1 Bring 6 cups water to a boil in a large nonreactive pot. Meanwhile, finely chop the rose hips in a food processor and transfer immediately to the boiling water.

2 Bring the mixture back to a boil and let stand for 15 minutes. Pour into a cheesecloth or other jelly bag, and let it drip overnight or until most of the liquid has come through. Reserve the pulp.

3 In the cleaned preserving pot, bring 3 cups fresh cold water to a boil. Stir in the pulp, turn off the heat, and let stand for 10 minutes. Pour into the cleaned jelly bag, and let drip for 2–3 hours.

4 Combine the two juices in a large bowl. Clean and wash the jelly bag thoroughly and pour the juices through once more.

5 Transfer the juices to the cleaned preserving pot and boil to reduce the liquid until it measures about 3¾ cups. Add the sugar and boil for another 5 minutes.

6 Pour into hot sterilized bottles, seal, and label.

INGREDIENTS

2¼lb (1kg) rose hips

1lb 5oz (600g) granulated sugar

COOKING AND STRAINING

To retain as much of the hips' vitamin content as possible, you must have the boiling water ready so you can plunge the hips into it as soon as you have chopped them. The rose hip and water mixture needs to be strained through the bag twice to ensure that all the tiny irritating fibers are removed.

Gathering wild chestnuts is a wonderful autumn pastime, but do check that you are allowed to do so. In many countries, even trees along main roads have owners who may object if you help yourself to their bounty. Don't worry if the nuts break when you are peeling them—they will still taste delicious. Serve with ice cream, or add to chocolate cakes and puddings.

Candied chestnuts

🕐 TAKES 60–80 MINUTES   🥘 MAKES 2¼LB (1KG)   🗄 KEEPS FOR 6 MONTHS

1 Make a small cut through the hard outer skin of each chestnut. Put the prepared nuts in a large saucepan, cover with water, and bring to a boil. Simmer for 10 minutes, then remove from the heat.

2 Using a slotted spoon, lift the chestnuts from the water one at a time, and peel off both the hard outer skin and the papery brown inner skin. From time to time, you will need to reheat the water, as the nuts peel much more easily when hot.

3 Put the sugar, 2 cups water, and vanilla bean in a stainless-steel or enameled saucepan, and stir over low heat for 5 minutes until the sugar has dissolved. Bring the mixture to a boil, then lower the heat and simmer for 3–4 minutes.

4 Add the chestnuts and boil for 10 minutes. Pour the syrup and nuts into a large heatproof glass or ceramic bowl, and let stand for at least 12 hours.

5 Split open the vanilla bean in half lengthwise. Scrape out the seeds, and add the seeds to the nuts and syrup.

6 Return the nuts and syrup to the cleaned preserving pot, bring to a boil, and cook for 1 minute. Transfer to the glass or ceramic bowl, and let stand for 24 hours.

7 Cook again in the cleaned preserving pot as in step 6, then ladle the mixture into hot sterilized jars, seal, and label.

INGREDIENTS

2¼lb (1kg) chestnuts

2¼lb (1kg) granulated sugar

1 vanilla bean

The nuts must pickled before the shells have started to form. To test this, prick each one with a needle at the end opposite the stem, and discard it if you feel any resistance. Each nut must also be pricked to allow the brine to sink in. A silver fork was once used because old-fashioned steel would taint the flavor, but modern stainless steel is fine. Serve with cheese or cold meats.

Pickled walnuts

⏱ NO COOKING   🍲 MAKES 3LB (1.5KG)   🥫 KEEPS FOR UP TO I YEAR

1. To make the brine, dissolve half the salt in 2 cups water in a large bowl. It helps the salt to dissolve if you heat a little of the water first, and then stir in the salt. Top with the remaining cold water and let cool. Brine should always be used cold to prevent bacterial growth.

2. Prick the walnuts all over with a fork, then add to the brine, ensuring that they are submerged: weight down with a plate if necessary. Let stand for 5 days.

3. Make a fresh batch of brine as above with the remaining salt and another 2 cups water. Drain the walnuts, submerge in the new brine, and let stand for another 7 days.

4. Drain the walnuts again and spread, in a single layer, on a tray to dry. I like to do this outside if the weather is warm. Turn the nuts often and let stand until they are uniformly black. This will take 2–3 days.

5. The day before you are due to pot the walnuts, make the spiced vinegar. Combine the vinegar and spices in a nonreactive saucepan, and bring to a boil. Add the sugar, stir well, and let stand for 24 hours to infuse.

6. When you are ready to pot the walnuts, drain the spiced vinegar into a clean nonreactive saucepan, and return to a boil. Pack the walnuts into hot sterilized jars, pushing them down well. Cover with the hot spiced vinegar, then cover the jars with vinegar-proof seals, and label. Let stand for at least 3 months to mature before using.

INGREDIENTS

1lb (450g) salt

2¼lb (1kg) walnuts, shelled and pricked with a silver or stainless-steel fork

FOR THE SPICED VINEGAR

4 cups malt vinegar

1 tbsp coriander seeds, crushed

12 allspice berries

2–3 red chiles, seeded if desired

2½oz (75g) light brown or muscovado sugar

Sloes are traditionally picked after the first frost. Given today's climatic vagaries, I put my sloes into the freezer for a couple of days. This helps the skins break down more easily. It also frees you to make the gin at a time convenient to you, as sloes freeze well for up to a year.

Sloe gin

🕐 NO COOKING   🍲 MAKES 2⅓ CUPS   🫙 KEEPS FOR 1–3 YEARS

1 Pick over the sloes, discarding any that are blemished or have become moldy. Now freeze airtight for at least overnight or up to 1 year.

2 When you are ready to make the liqueur, defrost the sloes. You now have two options for preparing them. You may prick them with a silver or stainless-steel fork (old-fashioned steel would taint the flavor). Alternatively, put them into the bowl of a food processor and pulse, turning the machine on and off, once or twice. I choose the latter method, but have friends who swear only hand-pricking each sloe makes the best gin.

3 Put the prepared sloes in a large china or glass bowl, and pour in the gin, reserving the bottle for later use. Stir in the sugar. Cover the bowl with two or three layers of plastic wrap, and let stand in a cool, dark place for 2–3 months.

4 Strain the gin through a double layer of scalded muslin or cheesecloth, then pour into the reserved bottle, seal, and label. Let the gin mature in a cool, dark place, for as long as you are able: 1 year is good; 3 years is even better.

INGREDIENTS

1lb 2oz (500g) frozen sloes (wild European plums)

3 cups (750ml) gin

3½oz (100g) granulated sugar

I always thought it wasteful to throw away the sloes used in the sloe gin recipe on p159, so now I reserve them to make this tangy jelly, which I like to serve with roasted game birds.

Sloe gin and juniper jelly

TAKES 75 MINUTES   MAKES 2¾LB (1.25KG)   KEEPS FOR 6–9 MONTHS

1   Put the sloes and 2 cups water in a nonreactive pot, bring to a boil, cover, and simmer for about 1 hour until the sloes are very soft. Spoon into a cheesecloth or other jelly bag and let drip overnight.

2   Put the resulting juice and the correct quantities of lemon juice, sugar, and pectin in the cleaned preserving pot. Bring to a boil, then cook at a full rolling boil for 4 minutes, stirring frequently. Test the mixture for a set.

3   When the jelly has reached the setting point, skim off any scum from the surface and add the juniper berries to the jelly. Boil for another minute, then ladle into hot sterilized jars, seal, and label.

INGREDIENTS

1lb 2oz (500g) sloes

10 juniper berries, crushed

FOR EACH 2⅓ CUPS JUICE

freshly squeezed juice of 1 lemon

1lb 2oz (500g) granulated sugar

4½oz (125g) liquid pectin

I first tasted this delicious jelly in Galway, Ireland. It's as good spooned onto your morning toast as it is eaten with roast lamb or venison, and is perfect with warm goat cheese.

Rowan jelly

TAKES 40 MINUTES   MAKES 4½LB (2KG)   KEEPS FOR 6–9 MONTHS

1   Put all the fruit in a large nonreactive pot, and just barely cover with water. Bring to a boil, then simmer for 20 minutes or until the fruit is soft. Let drip through a cheesecloth or other jelly bag overnight.

2   Measure the juice and weigh out the correct quantity of sugar. Add the juice and sugar to the cleaned preserving pot, and simmer over low heat for 10 minutes until the sugar has dissolved.

3   Increase the heat and cook at a full rolling boil for 5 minutes, then test for a set. When the jelly has reached the setting point, ladle into hot sterilized jars, seal, and label.

INGREDIENTS

4lb (1.8kg) rowan berries, rinsed and stems removed

3lb (1.35kg) cooking apples, peeled, cored, and quartered, or crabapples, peeled and cored

1lb (450g) granulated sugar for each 2⅓ cups juice

Horseradish grows wild in meadows and along roadsides, and is easily recognizable once you know what to look for. It's the root that is used, and it's hottest when freshly prepared.

Horseradish in vinegar

🕐 NO COOKING   🥣 MAKES 1LB (450G)   🥫 KEEPS FOR 6 WEEKS

1 Grate the horseradish. Take care when doing this, as the root will give off fiery fumes. I recommend using the fine grating disk of a food processor.

2 In a large bowl, sprinkle the salt over the horseradish and let stand for 1 hour. Rinse gently under cold running water, then squeeze dry using a clean dish towel. Pack into hot sterilized jars.

3 In a nonreactive saucepan, heat the vinegar to a boil, then pour over the horseradish to cover it completely. Cover the jars with vinegar-proof seals, label, and store in the refrigerator.

INGREDIENTS

1lb (450g) horseradish root, well scrubbed and peeled

1oz (30g) salt

10fl oz (300ml) white wine vinegar

Make sure that you are not picking in a restricted area when collecting samphire from the wild. Once you get home, wash it thoroughly to remove all traces of sand and mud.

Pickled samphire

🕐 NO COOKING   🥣 MAKES 1LB (450G)   🥫 KEEPS FOR 6 MONTHS

1 Arrange the samphire in layers in a deep bowl, sprinkling the salt between the layers. Let stand for 48 hours to draw out excess moisture. Rinse thoroughly under cold running water, then pat dry using clean dish towels.

2 Meanwhile, put the vinegar in a nonreactive saucepan and bring to a boil. Transfer to a clean bowl, add the spices, and let stand to infuse for 24–48 hours.

3 Pack the samphire into hot sterilized jars. Pour the spiced vinegar into the cleaned saucepan, bring to a boil, then pour into the jars. Be sure to fully immerse the samphire in the vinegar mixture. Cover with vinegar-proof seals, label, and let stand to mature for at least 2 weeks.

INGREDIENTS

12oz (350g) fresh samphire (salicornia), rinsed

1oz (30g) salt

2⅓ cups distilled malt vinegar, plus extra if needed

1 tbsp crushed coriander seeds

1 tbsp crushed fennel seeds

1 tbsp crushed white peppercorns

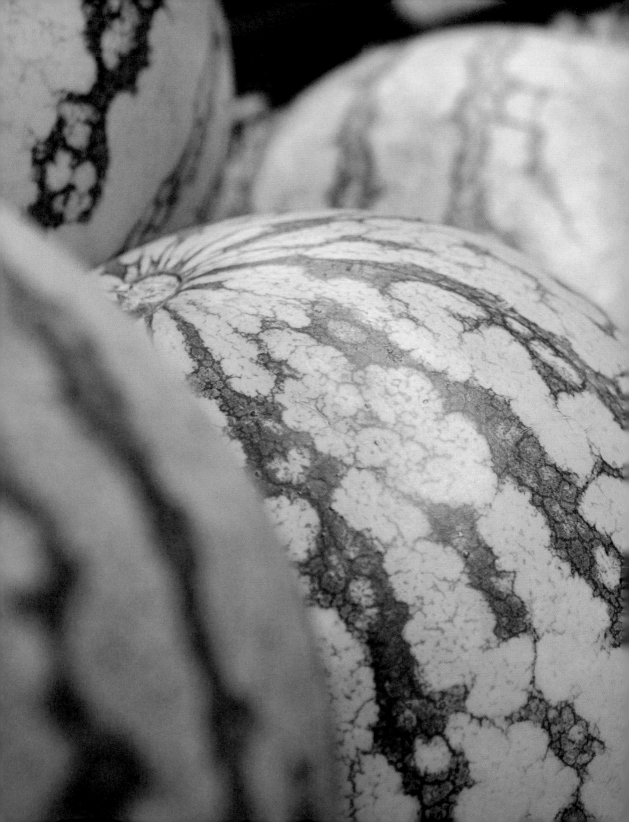

Tropical fruit

Bananas • Kiwi fruit • Mangoes
Melons • Passion fruit • Pineapple
Pomegranate • Watermelon

Use ripe, highly scented melons for this conserve. The usual pairing is to add ginger to the jam, but I like the more subtle notes of vanilla—or, for a real buzz, try some crushed star anise. Serve with shortbread, langues-de-chat or sugar cookies, or as an accompaniment to ice cream.

Melon and vanilla conserve

🕐 TAKES 30 MINUTES　🍲 MAKES 3LB (1.35KG)　🗃 KEEPS FOR 6–9 MONTHS

1　Arrange the melon in layers in a large china or glass bowl, sprinkling each layer with sugar and drizzling with the lemon juice. Let stand for 24 hours to draw the water from the fruit.

2　Strain the collected liquid into a nonreactive pot, reserving the melon cubes. Boil rapidly for 15–20 minutes to reduce the liquid by half.

3　Add the melon cubes, and simmer for another 4–5 minutes until the fruit is just tender.

4　Stir in the pectin, increase the heat, and cook at a full rolling boil for 2 minutes, then test for a set.

5　When the conserve has reached the setting point, skim off any scum from the surface, then stir in the vanilla seeds or crushed star anise. Let stand for 5 minutes to allow the jelly to thicken a little, so the melon cubes will not sink to the bottom when the conserve is in the jars. Ladle into hot sterilized jars, seal, and label.

INGREDIENTS

3lb 3oz (1.5kg) seeded melon flesh, chopped into ¾in (2cm) cubes

2¼lb (1kg) granulated sugar

freshly squeezed juice of 3 lemons

4½oz (125g) liquid pectin

seeds from one vanilla bean or 2 star anise seeds, crushed

CHOOSING YOUR MELON

Any variety of melon works well in this recipe, with the exception of watermelon. It is important, though, to choose melon that is ripe, scented, and flavorful. I sometimes add some finely chopped pistachio nuts to give the finished conserve a little texture.

Tropically scented, and like sunshine in color, this preserve is the perfect way to cheer up a dull winter's day. Serve with hot, crusty rolls and fresh coffee for a leisurely weekend breakfast.

Mango, passion fruit, and lime preserve

⏱ TAKES 30 MINUTES　　🍲 MAKES 3½LB (1.6KG)　　🍯 KEEPS FOR 6 MONTHS

1　Using a teaspoon, scoop the pulp from the passion fruit. Put in a nonreactive pot with the mango flesh and lime juice. Add 2 cups water, bring the mixture to a boil, and simmer for 20 minutes, or until the fruit is very soft.

2　Add the sugar, stirring until dissolved, then cook at a full rolling boil for 3–4 minutes, skimming off any scum that rises to the surface. This preserve produces a lot of scum, so you will need to skim regularly.

3　Stir in the pectin and continue to boil the mixture for 2 minutes, then test for a set.

4　When the conserve has reached the setting point, stir in the lime zest. Let the conserve settle for 5 minutes, then ladle into hot sterilized jars, seal, and label.

VARIATION
No limes on hand? Lemons or even blood oranges make a deliciously different preserve, with no sacrifice of flavor.

INGREDIENTS

8 large ripe passion fruit, halved

4 large ripe mangoes, about 2½lb (1.1kg) total weight, peeled, pitted, and coarsely chopped

finely grated zest and freshly squeezed juice of 4 large limes

1lb 10oz (750g) granulated sugar

4½oz (125g) liquid pectin

A rather unusual spread for your morning toast, this is also delicious spooned onto vanilla ice cream or natural yogurt, its fruity and slightly fiery flavor providing the perfect contrast.

Mango and chile jam

🕐 TAKES 20 MINUTES   🍲 MAKES 3LB 3OZ (1.5KG)   🫙 KEEPS FOR 6 MONTHS

1 Put the mango flesh in a food processor with the chiles, and reduce to a purée. Transfer the mixture to a nonreactive pot. Add 8fl oz (250ml) water, the sugar, and the lime juice.

2 Heat slowly for about 10 minutes, stirring to dissolve the sugar. Increase the heat and cook at a full rolling boil for 5 minutes.

3 Stir in the pectin. Return to a boil for 2 minutes, then test for a set. When the setting point has been reached, ladle the jam into hot sterilized jars, seal, and label.

INGREDIENTS

flesh from 4 ripe mangoes, about 1lb 10oz (750g)

3 red chiles, seeded

1lb 7oz (650g) granulated sugar

freshly squeezed juice of 3 limes

9oz (250g) liquid pectin

Sadly, these lovely vitamin-packed fruit lose some of their wonderful emerald color when cooked. Kiwi jam is excellent on buttered scones, or used as a filling for sponge cake.

Kiwi fruit jam

🕐 TAKES 10 MINUTES   🍲 MAKES 2¾LB (1.25KG)   🫙 KEEPS FOR 6 MONTHS

1 Cut out the hard cores of the fruit from the stem end. Put the kiwi fruit and apple juice in a food processor or blender, and process until you have a smooth purée. I leave the blacks seeds in, but you can sieve them out if you prefer.

2 Pour the purée into a nonreactive pot, and stir in the sugar. Cook over low heat for 5–8 minutes, stirring until the sugar has dissolved. Increase the heat and cook at a full rolling boil for 2 minutes.

3 Turn off the heat and stir in the pectin. Bring the mixture back to a boil and cook at a full rolling boil for 1 minute, then test for a set.

4 When the setting point has been reached, ladle the jam into hot sterilized jars, seal, and label.

INGREDIENTS

1lb 10oz (750g) kiwi fruit, peeled

8fl oz (250ml) apple juice

1lb 5oz (600g) granulated sugar

4½oz (125g) liquid pectin

Preserving tropical fruit

WHAT TO LOOK FOR

Heady with fragrance but often soft in texture, tropical fruits make wonderful jams and jellies, and marry particularly well with chiles for relishes and chutneys. Each fruit must be checked carefully for ripeness, as many will have traveled some distance to the market. Scent is often a good guide, as it is this perfume that you wish to capture in your preserve. Make sure there are no obvious blemishes and, cradling the fruit carefully in your hand, check that the flesh just yields to the touch.

MELONS Cradle the melon gently in your hands and press the stem end. It should yield slightly. Now take a good sniff—ripe fruit should also have a distinctive perfume.

WATERMELON These should be chosen by weight—they should feel heavy. Also check how perfect the rind is, as this is that part used in preserves.

MANGO Most varieties of mango are excellent for preserving. Larger fruit will yield more flesh, so look for these varieties. Choose unbruised, scented fruit with flesh that yields slightly.

PINEAPPLE The best test for ripeness here is to gently tug a leaf or two in the center of the crown. If they pull out easily, the pineapple is ripe. If not, it may be too green to use.

PASSION FRUIT As these are encased in a hard shell, testing for ripeness here is not by aroma or softness. Instead, you must look for a somewhat wrinkled skin, but without any mold.

KIWI FRUIT Choose large, unwrinkled fruit that yield a little when squeezed.

This lovely golden conserve makes a special breakfast treat, spread over hot buttered whole-wheat toast. Cardamom's warm fragrance has a special affinity with tropical fruit and gives a flavorful lift to the pineapple and apple base of this conserve.

Cardamom and pineapple conserve

🕐 TAKES 30 MINUTES   🍲 MAKES 2¾LB (1.25KG)   🫙 KEEPS FOR 6 MONTHS

1   Chop the pineapple flesh. I process mine in a food processor, pulsing the machine on and off, until it is well chopped, stopping just short of a purée. Alternatively, chop it finely using a sharp knife and a chopping board.

2   Put the pineapple and the chopped apples in a nonreactive pot with the sugar, cardamom seeds, lemon juice, and ⅓ cup water. Simmer over gentle heat for 10 minutes, stirring frequently, until all the sugar has dissolved.

3   Increase the heat and cook at a full rolling boil for about 20 minutes, stirring often, until the fruit is tender and the conserve is thick. Test the mixture for a set.

4   When the conserve has reached the setting point, ladle into hot sterilized jars, seal, and label.

VARIATION

For a change of flavor, add about 2 tablespoons freshly grated ginger along with the other ingredients.

INGREDIENTS

flesh of 2 ripe medium pineapples, about 1lb 10oz (750g)

1lb 2oz (500g) cooking apples, peeled, cored, and chopped

1lb 10oz (750g) granulated sugar

1 tsp cardamom seeds (removed from pods), crushed

freshly squeezed juice of 2 large lemons

Passion fruit has a wonderful but elusive flavor. Make this jelly in small batches and serve with scones and on sweet breads such as brioche.

Passion fruit jelly

🕐 TAKES 8 MINUTES   🍲 MAKES 1½LB (675G)   🥫 KEEPS FOR 6 MONTHS

1 Scoop the pulp from 10 of the passion fruit, and put the pulp into a nonreactive pot with the apple juice. Bring to a boil and simmer for 5 minutes. Spoon into a cheesecloth or other jelly bag and let drip overnight.

2 Measure the juice: you should have about 2 cups. Weigh out the correct quantity of sugar and add to the cleaned pot with the juice. Stir over low heat until the sugar has dissolved. Bring to a boil, then simmer for 2 minutes, skimming off any scum.

3 Turn off the heat and add the pulp from the remaining passion fruit. Stir well, increase the heat, and cook at a full rolling boil for about 1 minute. Test for a set.

4 When the jelly has reached the setting point, allow to cool for 5 minutes before ladling into hot sterilized jars. Seal and label.

INGREDIENTS

12 large ripe passion fruit, halved

2 cups unsweetened fresh apple juice

3½oz (100g) granulated sugar for each 3½fl oz (100ml) juice

This very simple jelly makes a wonderful jewel-like preserve. Combined with absolute simplicity of preparation, it's a combination that's hard to resist.

Pomegranate jelly

🕐 TAKES 5 MINUTES   🍲 MAKES 4½LB (2KG)   🥫 KEEPS FOR 6–9 MONTHS

1 Put all the ingredients in a nonreactive pot, and bring the mixture slowly to a boil.

2 When the sugar has dissolved, cook the mixture at a full rolling boil for 2 minutes, then test for a set.

3 Once the setting point has been reached, ladle the jelly into hot sterilized jars, seal, and label.

INGREDIENTS

4 cups best-quality pomegranate juice

2¼lb (1kg) granulated sugar

4½oz (125g) liquid pectin

freshly squeezed juice of 2 lemons

A sweet relish with a touch of chile, this is excellent with grilled chicken and firm fish such as tuna and swordfish. To tell whether a pineapple is ripe, try lifting it holding only one of the leaves in the middle of the crown—the leaf should pull easily from the fruit.

Pineapple and red onion relish

🕐 TAKES 35 MINUTES   🍲 MAKES 2¼LB (1KG)   🗄 KEEPS FOR 6–9 MONTHS

1   Using a sharp knife, cut the pineapple into wedges, removing the hard central core. Chop the flesh coarsely.

2   Put all the ingredients into a large nonreactive pot, and bring slowly to a boil, stirring often to ensure that the sugar dissolves.

3   Simmer the relish over medium heat for 25 minutes until the mixture thickens. To test whether the relish is ready, drag a wooden spoon through the mixture at the bottom of the pan. It should leave a clear path (see p22).

4   Ladle the pineapple relish into hot sterilized jars, cover with vinegar-proof seals, and label.

INGREDIENTS

flesh of 1 large or 2 ripe medium pineapples, 1lb 10oz (750g)

3 large red onions, chopped

2–6 red chiles, seeded if desired, and chopped

4 plump garlic cloves, crushed

2 tbsp fresh thyme leaves

10oz (300g) granulated sugar

1½ cups white wine vinegar

1 tsp salt

PAIRING FOR COLOR AND FLAVOR

I love the color red onions give this relish, but shallots also work well if you are willing to forgo the distinctive hue the onions impart—and you will not be sacrificing any of the flavor. You will need about 1lb 2oz (500g) peeled and chopped shallots in place of the onion.

This lovely preserve is delicious with hot buttered toast or muffins. It is economical, too, as it uses the usually discarded white watermelon rind, located between the pink flesh and the outer skin. Although a little tedious to prepare, it needs no great skill—just patience and a sharp knife.

Sweet watermelon preserve

⏱ TAKES 2 HOURS   🍲 MAKES 1LB 5OZ (600G)   🥫 KEEPS FOR 6–9 MONTHS

1 Using a small, sharp knife, cut the rind into strips about ½in (1cm) wide and about 1in (2.5cm) long.

2 To make the brine, put the salt and 2 cups water in a large china or glass bowl, stirring to dissolve the salt. Add the watermelon rind and let stand, covered, in a cool place for 24 hours.

3 Rinse the rind well under cold running water, and drain.

4 For the syrup, put the sugar and 4 cups water in a large nonreactive pot. Add the lemon rind. Bring the mixture to a boil, and add the drained watermelon rind. Simmer, partially covered, over the lowest possible heat for 1–2 hours until the rind is cooked through and translucent. Check the pot occasionally to ensure there is still some liquid; if not, add extra water.

5 Once the rind is tender and translucent, remove and discard the lemon peel, and spoon the rind carefully into hot sterilized jars. Spoon the syrup over the top.

6 Seal the jars, label, and store in a cool, dark place until needed.

VARIATION
You can use other citrus fruits instead of the lemon in this recipe. Both orange and lime work well, providing that distinctive citrus tang.

INGREDIENTS

1lb 5oz (600g) white watermelon rind from 1 large melon, peeled

2oz (60g) salt

FOR THE SYRUP

1lb 5oz (600g) granulated sugar

2 or 3 strips of lemon rind

Pickling watermelon rind is a clever way to use the enormous amount of rind per melon that would otherwise be discarded. Although the recipe takes several days to complete, once the rind is prepared the rest is simple. Serve with cold meats, cheeses, and sandwiches.

Watermelon rind pickle

🕐 TAKES 40–60 MINUTES   🍲 MAKES 1LB 5OZ (600G)   🫙 KEEPS FOR UP TO 1 YEAR

1 Using a small, sharp knife, cut the rind into strips about ½in (1cm) wide and about 1in (2.5cm) long.

2 To make the brine, put the salt and 2 cups water in a large china, glass, or earthenware bowl, stirring to dissolve the salt. Add the rind and refrigerate, covered, for 3 days.

3 Rinse the rind well under cold running water, and drain.

4 To make the pickling liquid, put the vinegar, 4 cups water, sugar, and spices in a large nonreactive saucepan. Bring the mixture to a boil, and add the watermelon rind.

5 Simmer the rind in the liquid for 40–60 minutes until the rind is cooked through and translucent. You may need to add more water as the mixture reduces.

6 Once the rind is tender, pack it into hot sterilized jars. Spoon the pickling liquid and spices overtop. Cover the jars with vinegar-proof seals, label, and store in a cool, dark place.

VARIATION
I love this combination of spices, but you can vary them to suit your taste, perhaps adding fresh ginger or even chopped fresh red chile.

INGREDIENTS

1lb 5oz (600g) white watermelon rind from 1 large melon, peeled

2oz (60g) salt

FOR THE PICKLING LIQUID

2 cups cider vinegar

250g (9oz) light brown or muscovado sugar

4in (10cm) cinnamon stick, roughly crushed

6 cloves, crushed

6 allspice berries, about ½ tsp, roughly crushed

Use any combination of dried fruits to suit your taste, but try to make it as varied as possible. This recipe takes very little time to cook, since the high proportion of dried fruit helps it thicken quickly. Serve with crackers or crusty bread, and firm mature cheese such as Cheddar.

Mango chutney

⏱ TAKES 30 MINUTES   🍲 MAKES ABOUT 4½LB (2KG)   🫙 KEEPS FOR UP TO 1 YEAR

1 Cut any of the larger dried fruits into ½in (1cm) pieces.

2 Transfer all of the dried fruit to a large heavy nonreactive pot, and stir in the remaining ingredients.

3 Bring the mixture to a boil, then reduce the heat and simmer for 30 minutes or until the chutney is thick, stirring occasionally to prevent it from sticking to the bottom of the pan.

4 While the chutney is still hot, ladle into hot sterilized jars, cover the jars with vinegar-proof lids, and label.

VARIATION
As this is an Indian-inspired chutney, some Asian spices can be added: a teaspoon of turmeric, some ground coriander, or a pinch of fenugreek.

INGREDIENTS

1½lb (675g) mixed dried fruits (such as apricots, figs, dates, peaches, and dark raisins)

3lb (1.35kg) mangoes, peeled, seeded, and chopped

1½lb (675g) light brown or muscovado sugar

2 large onions, chopped

6 plump garlic cloves, chopped

2oz (60g) fresh ginger, peeled and grated

1–2 dried red chiles, crushed

1 tbsp salt

4 cups cider or distilled malt vinegar

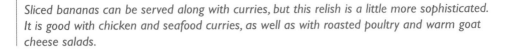

Sliced bananas can be served along with curries, but this relish is a little more sophisticated. It is good with chicken and seafood curries, as well as with roasted poultry and warm goat cheese salads.

Fresh banana relish

⏱ TAKES 20 MINUTES   🥘 MAKES 2LB (900G)   🥫 KEEPS FOR 3 MONTHS

1   Heat the oil in a large heavy pan over medium heat. Cook the onion for a few minutes until soft and translucent. Add the garlic and ginger, and cook for another 1–2 minutes until the onion is soft but not browned.

2   Add the cumin seeds and whole dried chiles, and cook for a few minutes to release their flavor. Now add the orange zest, raisins, vinegar, and sugar, and bring the mixture to a simmer.

3   Peel and thinly slice the bananas into pieces, and add these to the pan along with the salt. Simmer the mixture for 7–10 minutes until thick.

4   Ladle the relish into hot sterilized jars, cover the jars with vinegar-proof seals, and label. Store in the refrigerator.

VARIATION

For a delightful variation on this recipe, add 2oz (60g) unsweetened shredded coconut at the same time as the bananas and salt.

INGREDIENTS

2 tbsp vegetable oil

1 medium onion, finely chopped

1 plump garlic clove, crushed

1in (2.5cm) piece of fresh ginger, finely grated

1 tsp whole cumin seeds, crushed

3–4 dried red chiles

finely grated zest of 1 orange

2oz (60g) seedless dark raisins

½ cup white wine vinegar

4oz (115g) light brown or muscovado sugar

1lb (450g) slightly underripe bananas

½ tsp salt

Homemade fruit liqueurs provide a delicious end to a meal. I make several varieties so that I can offer friends a choice. They are all quite sweet and therefore work well when stored in the freezer or served 'on the rocks.' They are also delicious in syllabubs and drizzled over ice cream.

Passion fruit gin

🕐 NO COOKING   🥣 MAKES 3 CUPS   🥫 KEEPS FOR UP TO 18 MONTHS

1. Scrape the pulp from the passion fruit into a clean glass bowl. Now stir in the gin and sugar. (Keep the gin bottle for later use). Cover the bowl with a double layer of plastic wrap. Transfer to a cool, dark place.

2. Over the next 3–4 days, stir the liqueur occasionally until the sugar dissolves, then let stand for 4 weeks before straining into the reserved gin bottle. Store either in a cool, dark place or in the freezer.

INGREDIENTS

8 large ripe passion fruit

3 cups (750ml) gin (40% proof if possible)

9oz (250g) granulated sugar

This delightful cordial dates from Tudor times and makes a refreshing summer drink and a spicy addition to a white wine punch—it couldn't be easier to make.

Hypocras

🕐 TAKES 7 MINUTES   🥣 MAKES I PINT (600ML)   🥫 KEEPS FOR 6 MONTHS

1. Make a sugar syrup. Dissolve the sugar in 2⅓ cups water in a saucepan, and bring to a boil. Simmer for 5 minutes. Add the cinnamon, cardamom, and ginger, then cover the pan, remove from the heat, and let stand for 24 hours.

2. Strain the syrup through scalded muslin or cheesecloth into hot sterilized bottles, seal, and label. Store in a cool, dark place.

INGREDIENTS

8oz (225g) granulated sugar

4in (10cm) cinnamon stick, broken into pieces

2 tsp cardamom pods, crushed

2in (5cm) piece of fresh ginger, crushed

Chiles and spices

Caraway seeds • Chiles • Coriander seeds • Garlic
Ginger • Lemongrass • Mustard
Star anise • Tamarind

Hailing from Louisiana, this vibrant jelly is eaten with crackers and cream cheese. For extra bite, the chiles in this recipe retain their seeds, but they may be seeded if preferred.

Red pepper jelly

⏱ TAKES 10 MINUTES　　🥘 MAKES 3½LB (1.5KG)　　🥫 KEEPS FOR 6 MONTHS

1　Put the peppers and chiles in a blender or food processor, and chop finely, pulsing the machine on and off. Alternatively, chop by hand.

2　Transfer the chopped peppers and chiles to a deep, heavy nonreactive saucepan. Add the vinegar, and bring to a boil. Boil for 5 minutes, then let drip through a cheesecloth or other jelly bag overnight.

3　Pour the resulting liquid into the cleaned saucepan and add the sugar. Bring the mixture slowly to a boil over medium heat, stirring until the sugar has dissolved.

4　Add the pectin, increase the heat, and cook at a full rolling boil for 2 minutes, then test for a set.

5　When the jelly has reached the setting point, ladle into small sterilized jars and cover with vinegar-proof seals. Label the jars carefully, as you wouldn't want to spread this jelly on your morning toast!

INGREDIENTS

6 large red bell peppers, stems removed, halved, and seeded

12 red chiles, halved

2⅓ cups red wine vinegar

2¾lb (1.25kg) granulated sugar

9oz (250g) liquid pectin

CHOOSING YOUR CHILES

The version of this fiery jelly given here uses fresh red chiles, but you can use dried red chiles if you don't have fresh ones on hand. Simply soften the dried chiles in water overnight, then drain and proceed with the recipe as above.

Perfect for the garlic lover, this jelly is fabulous with lamb and pork dishes. I also like to serve it with warm goat cheese and young arugula leaves.

Garlic and green chile jelly

🕐 TAKES 50 MINUTES   🥣 MAKES 1¾LB (1.7KG)   🥫 KEEPS FOR 6 MONTHS

1 Using a food processor or blender, process the garlic and chiles to a paste. There is no need to peel the garlic or seed the chiles. Alternatively, pound to a paste with a mortar and pestle.

2 Transfer the paste to a heavy nonreactive pot with the apples and 4 cups water. Bring the mixture to a boil. Cover and simmer for about 40 minutes until all the ingredients are very soft. Spoon the mixture into a cheesecloth or other jelly bag, and let drip overnight.

3 Put the resulting liquid, vinegar, salt, and sugar in the cleaned preserving pot. Stir over low heat to dissolve the sugar, then cook at a full rolling boil for 5 minutes, or until the setting point has been reached. Ladle into hot sterilized jars, cover with vinegar-proof seals, and label.

INGREDIENTS

2 heads of fresh garlic, broken into cloves

6–8 green chiles

2¼lb (1kg) cooking apples, coarsely chopped

2 tbsp white wine vinegar

1 tsp salt

1lb (450g) granulated sugar

Another pretty apple-based jelly, this one is flecked with pieces of lemongrass and red chile.

Lemongrass and chile jelly

🕐 TAKES 40 MINUTES   🥣 MAKES 3½LB (1.5KG)   🥫 KEEPS FOR 6 MONTHS

1 Chop the apples and 2 of the chiles. Put the apples, chopped chile, 3 lemongrass stalks, and 6 cups water in a nonreactive pot. Simmer for 30 minutes until the apples are very soft. Spoon the mixture into a cheesecloth or other jelly bag, and let drip overnight.

2 Measure the resulting juice, and weigh out the correct quantity of sugar. Put in the cleaned preserving pot, and stir over low heat until the sugar has dissolved. Increase the heat and cook at a full rolling boil for 5 minutes until the setting point has been reached.

3 Chop the extra length of lemongrass and the remaining chiles. Add both to the jelly, and boil for 1 minute. Let the jelly cool for 5 minutes, then ladle into small sterilized jars, seal, and label.

INGREDIENTS

3lb 3oz (1.5kg) cooking apples

5 red chiles, seeded

3 bruised lemongrass stalks, plus 1 extra 1½in (4cm) length

1lb 2oz (500g) granulated sugar for each 2 cups juice

This rather interesting jelly has an amazing ginger kick. One of the joys of making it is that there is no need to peel the apples before cooking, as they will be strained through a jelly bag.

Ginger jelly

⏰ TAKES 50 MINUTES   🍲 MAKES 4½LB (2KG)   🥫 KEEPS FOR 6 MONTHS

1   Chop the apples and put in a nonreactive pot with 4 cups water and the fresh ginger, and bring to a boil. Cover and simmer for 30 minutes until the fruit is pulpy. Spoon the apple mixture into a cheesecloth or other jelly bag, and let drip for 6 hours or overnight.

2   Measure the resulting juice, and weigh out the correct quantity of sugar. Gently simmer the juice and sugar in the cleaned preserving pot, stirring until the sugar has dissolved. Increase the heat and cook at a full rolling boil for 10 minutes until the setting point is reached.

3   Skim off any scum from the surface, and stir in the preserved ginger and ginger wine, if using. Return to a boil, then turn off the heat and let stand for 10 minutes to allow the jelly to thicken slightly (to keep the ginger from sinking). Ladle into hot sterilized jars, seal, and label.

INGREDIENTS

4½lb (2kg) cooking apples

7oz (200g) fresh ginger, finely chopped

1lb 2oz (500g) granulated sugar for each 1½ cups water

5 or 6 pieces of stem ginger, preserved in syrup, drained and finely chopped

2fl oz (60ml) ginger wine (optional)

Spiked with sweet Spanish smoked paprika, this jam goes well with cheeses or cold meats.

Red pepper and chile jam

⏰ TAKES 15 MINUTES   🍲 MAKES 2¼LB (1KG)   🥫 KEEPS FOR 6 MONTHS

1   Remove the stems from the red peppers and chiles, then halve and seed them. Transfer to a blender or food processor, and chop finely. Alternatively, chop with a sharp knife.

2   Transfer to a deep, heavy nonreactive saucepan, and add the vinegar and sugar. Slowly bring the mixture to a boil, stirring until the sugar has dissolved. Boil rapidly for 5 minutes. Turn off the heat, and stir in the pectin. Stir in the pimenton dulce.

3   Turn on the heat and cook at a full rolling boil for 2 minutes, then test for a set. When the jam has reached the setting point, let it sit for 5 minutes to settle, then ladle into hot sterilized jars, seal, and label.

INGREDIENTS

5 large red bell peppers

4–8 red chiles

1½ cups white wine vinegar

2¾lb (1.25kg) granulated sugar

4oz (125g) liquid pectin

2 tbsp pimenton dulce (sweet smoked paprika)

Preserving with peppers

HOW TO USE PEPPERS

All peppers, both sweet and hot, belong to the Capsicum genus, which is part of the Solanaceae family that includes tomatoes, potatoes, and eggplants—as well as tobacco, the flowering plant datura, and deadly nightshade. Hot chile peppers are used to add a fiery flavor to food. This heat comes from the chemical capsaicin, which is concentrated in the pith. Removing the pith along with the seeds reduces the heat, while still allowing a good, full flavor.

Grading by heat

On the Scoville Scale, developed by Wilbur Scoville in 1912, peppers are graded as to the heat they impart, with chile peppers at one end of the scale and sweet peppers at the other. If you are not sure how hot a pepper is, use a small quantity—it is easier to add heat than take it out. Also remember that different chiles of the same variety can vary in capsaicin content. Green peppers and chiles are simply unripe red, yellow, or orange ones, and have a fresher flavor. Green chiles are milder than ripe ones, as capsaicin develops with ripeness: choose plump, unwrinkled ones for cooking. Red chiles can be used at all stages of ripeness and freshness. The riper and dryer the chiles are, the more concentrated the flavor.

- **Hot peppers** include habañero, Scotch bonnet, cayenne, and serrano chiles.
- **Medium peppers** include jalapeño, chipotle, and poblano.
- **Mild peppers** include bell or sweet peppers.

Hot peppers

SERRANO chiles are very hot and are available either fresh or dried.

SCOTCH BONNET chiles are among the hottest in the world, and should be used with care.

BIRD'S-EYE chiles are very high in capsaicin and have a good flavor.

INDIAN HOT chiles are the best choice for curries and vindaloo spice pastes.

Medium-hot peppers

Mild peppers

JALAPEÑO chiles are medium in heat; when dried and smoked, they are known as chipotles.

BELL PEPPERS, lowest of all on the capsaicin scale, come in various colors and are used for their rich sweet flavor.

TURKISH MARIMORA More usually found in specialty shops, these chiles have a good flavor and moderate kick.

ROMANO peppers are long and sweet, with a lovely flavor and little or no heat.

WESTLAND, or Dutch or Holland, chiles are medium in heat and good all-purpose chiles.

This lovely tangy chutney uses tamarind paste, available at well-stocked supermarkets or ethnic food stores, to add sharpness to the sweet tomatoes, while celery seeds provide the base note.

Tomato and tamarind chutney

🕐 TAKES 35 MINUTES 🍲 MAKES 3½LB (1.6KG) 🥫 KEEPS FOR 9 MONTHS

1 Put all the ingredients in a large nonreactive pot, and slowly bring the mixture to a boil. Simmer for 20–30 minutes, stirring often, then test to be sure that the chutney is thick enough. It will take longer to cook if the tomatoes are very juicy.

2 When the chutney has reached the desired consistency, ladle into hot sterilized jars, cover the jars with vinegar-proof seals, and label.

VARIATION
You can replace the celery seed used in this chutney with crushed cardamom seeds, and add some finely grated orange zest, too.

INGREDIENTS

2¼lb (1kg) tomatoes, coarsely chopped

4 large onions, finely chopped

5oz (150g) celery, finely chopped

4 red chiles, seeded if desired, and chopped

6 plump garlic cloves, crushed

5oz (150g) golden raisins (sultanas)

2 tbsp tamarind paste

1 tsp celery seed

10oz (300g) granulated sugar

1 tbsp salt

14fl oz (400ml) cider vinegar

This spicy mix comes from North Africa, where it is commonly rubbed onto fish. I also like to use it on white meats such as pork and chicken. It makes a tasty marinade for tofu, too.

Chermoula

🕐 TAKES 5 MINUTES   🍲 MAKES 10OZ (300G)   🫙 KEEPS FOR 4 WEEKS

1 Crush the garlic. Grind the cumin and coriander seeds in a spice mill or clean coffee grinder, or use a mortar and pestle.

2 Put all the ingredients in a small saucepan. Add ½ cup water, and bring to a boil. Simmer for 4–5 minutes until reduced by half.

3 Pour the mixture into a hot, sterilized jar, cover with a vinegar-proof seal, and label. Store in the refrigerator until needed.

INGREDIENTS

4 garlic cloves

3 tsp cumin seeds

4 tbsp coriander seeds

2 tbsp pimenton dulce (sweet smoked paprika)

I tsp cayenne pepper

3½fl oz (100ml) red wine vinegar

freshly squeezed juice of 3 lemons

⅓ cup olive oil

Found throughout North Africa, this fiery sauce should be used in small doses! A traditional accompaniment to tagines, it can also spice up anything from casseroles to cornbreads.

Harissa

🕐 NO COOKING   🍲 MAKES ½ CUP   🫙 KEEPS FOR 4 MONTHS

1 Soften the chiles in water for 30 minutes, then drain.

2 Process the chiles in a food processor or blender with the garlic, spices, and enough of the 4 tbsp olive oil to make a soft paste. Alternatively, pound the chiles, garlic, spices, and salt to a paste using a mortar and pestle, then add the oil.

3 Spoon into a hot sterilized jar, cover with extra oil, seal, and label. Store the harissa in the refrigerator.

INGREDIENTS

2oz (60g) dried red chiles

4 garlic cloves

I tsp caraway seeds

I tsp coriander seeds

½ tsp salt

4 tbsp olive oil, plus extra to cover

I will forever associate this classic relish with hot dogs, hamburgers, and baseball games. Try it with other foods, too—as well as other pastimes ... I find it especially good with chicken or grilled fish dishes.

Corn and chile relish

TAKES 40 MINUTES   MAKES 2LB (900G)   KEEPS FOR 6–9 MONTHS

1 Put all the ingredients except the salt in a large nonreactive pot, and cook the mixture over low heat, stirring occasionally, until the sugar has dissolved.

2 Bring to a boil, then reduce the heat to low and simmer for 20 minutes until the relish has thickened slightly. Test that it has achieved the right consistency: the relish is ready when there is still only a little loose liquid in the pan. Since this is a chunky relish, it will be a little more liquidy than a chutney.

3 Add the salt and stir the chutney until the salt has dissolved.

4 Pot the relish into hot sterilized jars, cover with vinegar-proof seals, and label.

VARIATION
Green peppers and green chiles, being milder in flavor, give a change both to the appearance and to the taste of this relish.

INGREDIENTS

1lb 2oz (500g) corn kernels, cut from 4–5 cobs

2 red chiles, seeded if desired, and chopped

4oz (115g) seeded and chopped red pepper

4oz (115g) chopped celery

4oz (115g) chopped red onion

6oz (175g) granulated sugar

freshly squeezed juice of 1 large lemon

10fl oz (300ml) white wine vinegar

1 tsp mustard powder

½ tsp celery seed

2 tbsp salt

This is my favorite barbecue sauce. Remember that it's very sticky-sweet and so has a tendency to burn easily. When using it, baste onto the food toward the end of cooking.

Smoky barbecue sauce

TAKES 15 MINUTES   MAKES 3 CUPS   KEEPS FOR 6 WEEKS

1   Put all the ingredients in a large nonreactive saucepan, and whisk together until smooth. Slowly bring the mixture to a boil, whisking occasionally, until the sugar has dissolved.

2   Simmer the sauce over medium-low heat for 10–15 minutes until it thickens and becomes syrupy.

3   Pour into hot, sterilized bottles, seal with vinegar-proof lids, and label. Store the sauce in the refrigerator.

VARIATION

If you can find liquid smoke in your local market, add about 1 tablespoon to the mix for a truly smoky flavor. When diluted by 50 percent with water, this sauce is ideal for oven-baked spare ribs.

INGREDIENTS

2⅓ cups orange juice

6oz (175g) light brown or muscovado sugar

7fl oz (200ml) Worcestershire sauce

7fl oz (200ml) soy sauce

5fl oz (150ml) cider vinegar

10fl oz (300ml) tomato ketchup

4 garlic cloves, crushed

¼ cup prepared mustard

hot pepper sauce, such as Tabasco, to taste

freshly ground black pepper, to taste

This Indonesian take on soy sauce is much more complex than other East and Southeast Asian varieties. It makes an excellent barbecue marinade, and a great addition to stir-fries.

Ketjap manis

🕐 TAKES 15 MINUTES　　🍲 MAKES 14FL OZ (400ML)　　🍶 KEEPS FOR 6 MONTHS

1　Put all the ingredients in a heavy nonreactive saucepan. Place over low heat and simmer slowly, stirring, until the sugar has dissolved.

2　Increase the heat and continue to simmer for 5 minutes, stirring often until the mixture thickens and becomes syrupy. Remember that it will thicken slightly as it cools.

3　Have ready a sieve lined with scalded muslin or cheesecloth. When the sauce is thickened to your liking, strain it through the sieve, then ladle into hot sterilized jars, seal, and label. Store in either a cool, dark place or the refrigerator until needed.

INGREDIENTS

2 cups soy sauce

9oz (250g) light brown or muscovado sugar

9oz (250g) molasses

4 garlic cloves, crushed

2in (5cm) piece of fresh ginger, finely chopped

2–3 star anise, crushed

1 tbsp coriander seeds

This sauce is delicious with roast duck, hot dogs, and barbecue dishes. For a more textured sauce, replace the mustard powder with 7oz (200g) coarse-grain prepared mustard.

Orange and honey mustard sauce

🕐 TAKES 15 MINUTES　　🍲 MAKES 1LB 5OZ (600G)　　🍶 KEEPS FOR 3 MONTHS

1　Put the garlic and salt in a bowl, and mash together until you have a smooth purée. Strip the leaves from the thyme sprigs.

2　Transfer the garlic purée and thyme leaves to a heavy nonreactive saucepan. Add the remaining ingredients and bring the mixture to a boil, whisking to blend in the mustard powder.

3　Boil rapidly for about 10 minutes until the sauce reduces and thickens. It should be the consistency of heavy cream.

4　Ladle into hot sterilized jars, cover with vinegar-proof seals, and label. This sauce may separate, so shake the jar before using.

INGREDIENTS

4 garlic cloves, crushed

1 tbsp salt

3 sprigs of fresh thyme

juice of 6 oranges

1¾oz (50g) English mustard powder, such as Colman's

7fl oz (200ml) cider vinegar

12oz (350g) honey

A surplus of chiles prompted me to make this dipping sauce for the first time. It's so easy to do and has such a superior flavor to the ready-made version that I always make my own now.

Sweet chile dipping sauce

⏱ TAKES 10–15 MINUTES   🍲 MAKES 3 CUPS   🥫 KEEPS FOR 6 MONTHS

1 Put the vinegar and sugar in a large deep nonreactive saucepan and slowly bring to a boil, stirring until the sugar has dissolved.

2 Increase the heat and boil rapidly for 5 minutes until the mixture becomes syrupy.

3 Add the chiles and salt and cook for another 3–4 minutes. Watch carefully, as the mixture will bubble up at first.

4 Ladle into hot sterilized jars, cover with vinegar-proof seals, and label.

INGREDIENTS

4 cups rice vinegar

1lb 14oz (850g) granulated sugar

12oz (350g) red chiles, stemmed and finely chopped with pith and seeds

2 tbsp salt

This Japanese barbecue sauce is delicious with pork, chicken, tofu, or shrimp. Mirin is a rice wine and is available at well-stocked supermarkets and Asian food stores.

Teriyaki sauce

⏱ TAKES 10 MINUTES   🍲 MAKES 2 CUPS   🥫 KEEPS FOR 2 MONTHS

1 Put all the ingredients in a nonreactive saucepan, and slowly bring to a boil. Once the sugar has dissolved, simmer the sauce for 5 minutes.

2 Pour into a sterilized bottle and seal. Store in the refrigerator.

INGREDIENTS

1 cup soy sauce

1 cup mirin

2oz (60g) granulated sugar

The choice of crunchy or smooth peanut butter for this recipe is a matter of taste—I prefer the coarser texture that the crunchy type provides. Serve with barbecued chicken, pork, or fish.

Chile, peanut, and garlic sauce

TAKES 10 MINUTES   MAKES 1¾LB (800G)   KEEPS FOR 6 WEEKS

1 Finely chop the garlic. Seed the chiles, if desired, for a milder flavor, then chop.

2 Put all the ingredients in a nonreactive saucepan and whisk well to combine. Bring to a boil, then simmer for 5 minutes. Be careful, as the mixture can bubble up, spattering hot sauce onto your hands.

3 When the mixture has thickened to the consistency of thick custard, ladle into hot sterilized jars, cover with vinegar-proof seals, and label. Store in the refrigerator.

INGREDIENTS

8 garlic cloves

3–4 large red chiles

9oz (250g) peanut butter

9oz (250g) light brown or muscovado sugar

1¼ cups red wine vinegar

1 tsp salt

As useful at Christmas as on summer picnics, this is a pantry favorite to make year-round. Serve with pâtés, game terrines, or a hard cheese such as mature Cheddar.

Sweet and sour pickled figs

TAKES 10 MINUTES   MAKES 1LB 5OZ (600G)   KEEPS FOR UP TO 1 YEAR

1 Remove the stems from the figs and slice thinly.

2 Put the figs in a large nonreactive saucepan with the sugar, chiles, and vinegar, and warm gently over low heat, stirring until the sugar has dissolved.

3 Simmer the mixture gently for 3–5 minutes until the figs begin to soften. If the mixture is very dry, add more vinegar.

4 Let cool a little before ladling into hot sterilized jars, covering with vinegar-proof seals, and labeling. Let the figs mature for about 4 weeks before using.

INGREDIENTS

1lb 2oz (500g) good-quality dried figs

3oz (85g) dark brown or muscovado sugar

2–3 dried chiles, finely chopped

1¼ cups red wine vinegar, plus extra if needed

A wonderful addition to any cook's pantry, these peppers are as beautiful to look at as they are delicious to eat. Serve with antipasti, or slice into salads for extra color and flavor.

Pickled sweet peppers

⏱ TAKES 30 MINUTES   🍲 MAKES I LB 5OZ (600G)   🫙 KEEPS FOR 3 MONTHS

1 Roast the peppers under a hot broiler or on a barbecue grill until the skins are blistered and black all over. Put in a glass or china bowl while hot, cover with plastic wrap, and let cool.

2 When cool enough to handle, rub off the blackened skins and seed the peppers. Slice thinly and pack into hot sterilized jars.

3 Meanwhile, combine the vinegar, sugar, pepper flakes, and salt in a nonreactive saucepan and bring to a boil. Simmer the mixture for 10 minutes or until reduced by half.

4 Pour the boiling mixture over the peppers, making sure that they are completely submerged, and adding extra vinegar if necessary. Cover with vinegar-proof seals, label, and store in a cool, dark place for up to 6 weeks before using. Once opened, store in the refrigerator.

INGREDIENTS

4 large ripe red peppers

1½ cups white wine vinegar, plus extra if needed

3 tbsp granulated sugar

large pinch of crushed red hot pepper flakes

I tsp salt

Hot and spicy, this is just the thing to kickstart a Bloody Mary. Store the vodka in the freezer, and serve in shot glasses or as part of a vibrant cocktail.

Chile pepper vodka

⏱ NO COOKING   🍲 MAKES 3 CUPS   🫙 KEEPS FOR UP TO I YEAR

1 Add the chiles to the vodka. Shake well every day for I week.

2 Transfer the bottle to the freezer. The vodka is ready to use when it is icy cold.

INGREDIENTS

3–10 red chiles, seeded if desired, and chopped

I bottle (750ml) vodka

Served in sushi bars worldwide, this pretty pickle works well with fish and chicken dishes. Chopped finely, it can be mixed into Asian salad dressings or folded into freshly cooked rice with a touch of wasabi paste, to serve with steamed fish.

Pink pickled ginger

🕐 TAKES 1¼ HOURS   🍲 MAKES 1LB 2OZ (500G)   🗄 KEEPS FOR 4 MONTHS

1   Peel the ginger if necessary, then slice it thinly and put the slices in a large bowl.

2   Sprinkle the ginger with the salt and toss to coat thoroughly. Let the mixture sit for 1 hour, then rinse the slices with cold water and pat dry using paper towels.

3   Pack the ginger into hot sterilized jars.

4   Put the vinegar and sugar in a nonreactive saucepan. Heat gently, stirring until the sugar has dissolved. Bring to a boil, then pour the vinegar over the ginger while still hot.

5   Cover the jars with vinegar-proof seals, label, and let cool before storing in the refrigerator.

INGREDIENTS

1lb 2oz (500g) fresh young ginger

1 tbsp salt

1 cup rice wine vinegar

4oz (115g) superfine sugar

PREPARING THE GINGER

As it matures, the pickled ginger turns a pretty pink. To get this effect, however, you need to use fresh young ginger. You can find this in Asian markets or specialty food stores. Very young ginger does not need peeling. If it is slightly older, I find the easiest way to remove the skin is to scrape it off with a teaspoon.

Winter citrus

Clementines • Grapefruit • Kumquats
Lemons • Limes
Seville oranges • Sweet oranges

This is a real old-fashioned favorite. If you can find organic Seville oranges and ginger, use them. This recipe makes a large quantity of marmalade, but it stores well, so will not be wasted.

Orange and ginger marmalade

🕐 TAKES 90 MINUTES   🍲 MAKES 10LB (4.4KG)   📦 KEEPS FOR UP TO 1 YEAR

1 Rinse the oranges under warm running water, then put them, whole, along with the fresh ginger and 8 cups water, in a large nonreactive pot. Bring the mixture to a boil. Cover with a lid and simmer for 40–50 minutes until the fruit is soft.

2 Using a slotted spoon, remove the ginger and fruit from the pan, and set aside. Measure the cooking liquid and add enough water to make a total of 6 cups. Add the sugar and let it start to dissolve off the heat.

3 Cut the reserved oranges in half, and scrape all the seeds and pith into a bowl. Enclose the pith and seeds in a square of muslin or cheesecloth and tie securely. Thinly slice the peel. Add the muslin bag, and the peel to the pot.

4 Bring the mixture to a boil, then simmer for 10 minutes. Add the ginger syrup and the preserved ginger. Continue to cook for another 30 minutes, or until the marmalade has reached the setting point. Ladle into hot sterilized jars, seal, and label. Remove and discard the bag of seeds.

INGREDIENTS

2¾lb (1.25kg) Seville or other bitter oranges, scrubbed

4oz (115g) fresh ginger, crushed

3lb 3oz (1.5kg) unrefined (raw) sugar

1 7oz (200g) jar stem ginger, preserved in syrup, drained and thinly sliced

ENSURING SOFT PEEL

For marmalade lovers, the delight is in the peel found in this traditional favorite. It's important to be patient and always cook the fruit fully before you add the sugar. Otherwise the peel will toughen, and the finished preserve suffers as a result.

This takes a little effort, but the result is fabulous, sharp, and tangy—and perfect for morning toast and for those who prefer a lighter marmalade, rather than the traditional chunky type.

Lemon marmalade

⏱ TAKES 80 MINUTES   🍲 MAKES 3LB (1.35KG)   🥫 KEEPS FOR UP TO 1 YEAR

1 Pare the peel from the lemons as thinly as possible, leaving behind as much of the white pith as you can. The easiest method is to use a swivel-bladed vegetable peeler. Thinly slice the peel, and put in a large saucepan with 3 cups water.

2 Bring to a boil, cover, and simmer for 30–40 minutes until the peel is very soft. Set aside to cool.

3 Meanwhile, coarsely chop the peeled lemons and put the fruit, seeds and all, in a nonreactive pot with 3 cups water. Bring to a boil, cover, and simmer for about 1 hour until the fruit is very soft.

4 Strain the liquid from the sliced peel into the pot, reserving the peel. Spoon the mixture into a cheesecloth or other jelly bag, and let drip overnight.

5 Measure the juice: you should have about 4 cups. Put this in the cleaned preserving pot with the sugar. Heat gently until the sugar has dissolved, then increase the heat and cook at a full rolling boil for 5–10 minutes until the marmalade has reached the setting point.

6 Skim off any scum that rises to the surface, then stir in the reserved peel. Return to a boil and cook for 1 minute. Let stand for 5 minutes before ladling into hot sterilized jars, sealing, and labeling.

INGREDIENTS

2¼lb (1kg) lemons, scrubbed

2¼lb (1kg) granulated sugar

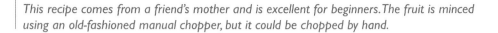

This recipe comes from a friend's mother and is excellent for beginners. The fruit is minced using an old-fashioned manual chopper, but it could be chopped by hand.

Easy everyday marmalade

🕐 TAKES 75 MINUTES   🍲 MAKES 5½LB (2.5KG)   🫙 KEEPS FOR UP TO 1 YEAR

1   Put the fruit and 6 cups water in a nonreactive pot, cover, and simmer for 50–60 minutes until the fruit is very soft. Remove from the heat, lift out the fruit, and set aside to cool. Meanwhile, measure the liquid and add enough to make 5 cups. Return to the pan and stir in the sugar.

2   Halve the fruit and squeeze out the seeds. Tie the seeds securely in a square of muslin. Mince or chop the peel and flesh. Add to the pot with the bag of seeds. Stir over low heat until the sugar has dissolved.

3   Increase the heat and cook at a full rolling boil for 10–15 minutes until the marmalade has reached the setting point. Remove and discard the bag of seeds, and ladle the marmalade into hot sterilized jars, seal, and label.

INGREDIENTS

7 Seville or other bitter oranges, scrubbed

2 sweet oranges, scrubbed

1 large lemon, scrubbed

3lb (1.35kg) granulated sugar

This marmalade is usually described as traditional or vintage as it has a rich caramel flavor, a chunky cut, and a good kick of whisky. No whisky in the house? Brandy works just as well!

Whisky marmalade

🕐 TAKES 90 MINUTES   🍲 MAKES 9LB (2.7KG)   🫙 KEEPS FOR UP TO 1 YEAR

1   Put the oranges and 8 cups water in a nonreactive pot, cover, and simmer for 50–60 minutes until the fruit is very soft. Remove from the heat, lift out the fruit, and cool. Measure the liquid and add enough water to make 6 cups. Stir in the sugar.

2   Halve the oranges and scoop out the flesh and seeds. Tie the seeds securely in a square of muslin. Chop the peel coarsely. Add to the pan with the muslin bag. Stir over low heat until the sugar has dissolved.

3   Increase the heat and cook at a full rolling boil for 10 minutes until the marmalade has reached the setting point. Cool for 10 minutes. Stir in the whisky, ladle into hot sterilized jars, seal, and label.

INGREDIENTS

3lb 3oz (1.5kg) Seville or other bitter oranges, scrubbed

3lb 3oz (1.5kg) light brown or muscovado sugar

¼ cup whisky

Pink and ruby grapefruit make a lovely preserve. They often have thin peel, but if the white pith is very thick, pare some away before chopping.

Pink grapefruit marmalade

🕐 TAKES 1½ HOURS　　🍲 MAKES 3½LB (1.6KG)　　🗄 KEEPS FOR UP TO 1 YEAR

1　Cut the fruit in half and carefully squeeze out all the juice, straining it into a large bowl. Reserve the seeds. Store the juice and seeds, covered, in the refrigerator until needed.

2　Using a sharp knife, cut the shells of the grapefruit and lemons into thin strips. Put these in a large china or glass bowl, and cover with 6 cups water. Let stand for 24 hours.

3　Enclose the reserved seeds in a muslin or cheesecloth bag and tie securely. Put the fruit and water into a nonreactive pot with the reserved juice and the bag of seeds. Bring to a boil, then simmer for 60 minutes or until the peel is very soft. You must be able to cut it easily with a wooden spoon.

4　Stir in the sugar, and simmer over low heat until it has dissolved. If any scum rises to the surface, skim it off as the mixture boils: you may need to do this several times. Now increase the heat and cook at a full rolling boil for 20–30 minutes, then test for a set.

5　When the marmalade has reached the setting point, let it stand for 5 minutes, then ladle into hot sterilized jars, seal, and label.

VARIATION

Yellow grapefruit work well here. When available, try to buy best-quality large fruit with no skin blemishes, to make sure you end up with a superior preserve.

INGREDIENTS

3 pink- or red-fleshed grapefruit, scrubbed

2 large lemons, scrubbed

3lb (1.35kg) granulated sugar

Preserving citrus fruits

CHOOSING AND COOKING

Oranges, lemons, and limes—where would cooking be without these wonderful taste-enhancing fruits that add color, flavor, and piquancy to such a variety of foods, both sweet and savory? Add to this familiar trio other lesser-used citrus varieties such as grapefruit, mandarins, and kumquats, and you have an enticing range of basic ingredients with which to make jams, relishes, and other preserves.

What to look for

Choose ripe fruit without bruises or blemishes. Do not be misled by the color of the skin: this is not always a good guide, since many citrus fruits are fully ripe when the skins are still quite green.

Softening the peel

When cooking citrus fruits, it is necessary to boil them in plenty of water before adding any sugar so that the peel is thoroughly cooked, or it may become tough and spoil the finished preserve. Both lemons and limes take longer to cook, so allow plenty of time. Lemons are commonly used to add acid to low-acid preserves. Their juice is best used freshly squeezed. Most lemons yield 3 tablespoons (1½fl oz/45ml) or so of juice.

MAKE LIQUID PECTIN at home by boiling the shells left over once the juice has been used (see p15). The shells can be frozen until needed. Commercial pectin is made by boiling citrus skins in water to extract the pectin, then either bottling the resulting liquid or drying it to form a powder.

GRATE THE ZEST and add to marmalades. It may be grated coarsely or thinly sliced for the classic chunky marmalade, or more finely for a more delicate preserve.

ORANGES AND LEMONS, the most familiar of all citrus fruits, are commonly sold with waxed skins to extend their shelf life and aid appearance. Before cooking, scrub the skins well to remove the wax coating. Alternatively, buy unwaxed organic citrus fruit.

RESERVE THE PITH AND SEEDS when preparing the fruit; these contain most of the pectin. Secure them in a muslin bag, and boil along with the peel.

COOK CITRUS PEEL thoroughly until soft; if it is still tough, it may spoil the finished preserve.

No shreds of zest this time, but a really tart, fragrant marmalade. Use ripe limes that have just begun to turn yellowish-brown. This marmalade reaches the setting point quickly, so be prepared.

Lime jelly marmalade

🕐 TAKES 30 MINUTES   🍲 MAKES 3LB (1.35KG)   🥫 KEEPS FOR 6 MONTHS

1 Cut the limes in half and squeeze out the juice. Reserve the shells and the juice.

2 Finely chop the reserved shells in a food processor, or chop by hand. Put in a large nonreactive pot with 4 cups water. Bring the mixture to a boil, cover, and simmer for 20 minutes. Spoon into a jelly bag along with the reserved juice. Let drip overnight.

3 Pour the liquid into the cleaned preserving pot, and add the sugar. Warm over low heat, stirring, until the sugar has dissolved. Increase the heat and cook at a full rolling boil for about 1 minute, then test for a set. When the marmalade has reached the setting point, ladle into hot sterilized jars, seal, and label.

INGREDIENTS

1lb 10oz (750g) ripe limes, scrubbed

2¼lb (1kg) granulated sugar

Kumquats have the odd distinction in the citrus family of having pith that is sweeter than the fruit inside. They make a rather sophisticated preserve, suited to the finest breakfast tables.

Kumquat marmalade

🕐 TAKES 40 MINUTES   🍲 MAKES 2¾LB (1.25KG)   🥫 KEEPS FOR 6 MONTHS

1 Cut the kumquats into thin slices. Remove the seeds, letting the juice drip into a bowl. Tie the seeds securely in a square of muslin or cheesecloth. Put in a heavy nonreactive pot with the kumquats and any juices, the lemon juice and zest, and 14fl oz (400ml) water. Cover the pan, and simmer for 25 minutes until the fruit is very tender.

2 Squeeze as much juice as possible out of the bag of seeds, then discard the bag. Add the sugar, and stir over low heat until the sugar has dissolved. Increase the heat and cook at a full rolling boil for 5 minutes, then test for a set.

3 When the marmalade has reached the setting point, ladle into hot sterilized jars, seal, and label.

INGREDIENTS

1lb 2oz (500g) kumquats

finely grated zest and freshly squeezed juice of 1 lemon

1lb 2oz (500g) granulated sugar

Sweeter than most, clementine marmalade makes a lovely, rich breakfast treat. Although the fruit has very thin skin, it will still need some precooking to make a tender preserve.

Clementine marmalade

🕐 TAKES 40 MINUTES   🍲 MAKES 3LB (1.35KG)   🗄 KEEPS FOR 6 MONTHS

1 Discard any seeds from the clementines, then process in a food processor until the skins and flesh are finely chopped, or chop by hand. Turn the fruit into a nonreactive pot and add 4 cups water and the lemon juice. Bring to a boil and simmer for 7–10 minutes until the rind is soft.

2 Add the sugar, and stir until it has dissolved completely. Increase the heat and cook at a full rolling boil for 25 minutes, then test for a set.

3 When the marmalade has reached the setting point, ladle into hot sterilized jars, seal, and label.

INGREDIENTS

1lb 10oz (750g) clementines or other mandarin oranges, washed and halved

freshly squeezed juice of 2 lemons

1lb 10oz (750g) granulated sugar

Homemade lemon curd is amazing. I make mine with heavy cream, so this version is stored in the refrigerator, where it will keep, unopened, for 3–4 weeks.

Lemon curd

🕐 TAKES 25 MINUTES   🍲 MAKES 1LB 10OZ (750G)   🗄 KEEPS FOR 1 MONTH

1 Combine all the ingredients in a large, wide nonreactive pan—I use a deep non-stick frying pan. Simmer the mixture over low heat, stirring constantly with a wooden spoon, for 15–20 minutes until it begins to coat the back of the spoon. You must not let the mixture boil, so use very low heat and never leave the pan unattended.

2 When the curd is as thick as homemade mayonnaise, ladle into hot sterilized jars and let cool for 5 minutes before sealing and labeling. Let the curd cool completely, then store in the refrigerator until needed. Once opened, consume within 1 week.

INGREDIENTS

5 large eggs, beaten

7oz (200g) superfine sugar

¾ cup heavy cream

finely grated zest and freshly squeezed juice of 3 scrubbed or unwaxed lemons

Oranges and lemons are a more common combination for this particular recipe, but limes add more fragrance than lemons. If the limes are very lacking in juice, add the juice of 1 lemon. This curd goes well on hot buttered biscuits or English muffins, or spoon it over meringues.

Orange and lime curd

(L) TAKES 40 MINUTES   MAKES 1LB 5OZ (600G)   KEEPS FOR 3 MONTHS

1 Using a very fine grater, grate the zest from the fruit, then squeeze out the juice.

2 Mix together the zests and juices in a wide heavy nonreactive saucepan. Add the sugar, butter, and eggs. Place the pan over low heat and simmer, whisking gently until the butter has melted.

3 Continue to cook the curd over low heat, stirring constantly with a wooden spoon to ensure the curd does not stick to the pan. Watch it constantly, and remove from the heat as soon as it thickens. It should be the consistency of half-and-half or light cream. If the mixture is beginning to curdle, turn it into a large cold bowl, and whisk vigorously: this may save it. Alternatively, cook in a double boiler. This will take longer, but decreases the risk of curdling.

4 After removing the curd from the heat, stir again. If you feel the curd isn't quite thick enough, return to the heat and cook for a little longer, remembering that it will thicken further as it cools.

5 Once the mixture has achieved the desired consistency, ladle into hot sterilized jars, seal, and label. Store in the refrigerator. Once opened, consume within 1 week.

INGREDIENTS

3 large oranges, scrubbed

2 large limes, scrubbed

7oz (200g) granulated sugar

4½oz (125g) unsalted butter, diced

2 large eggs, beaten

This is a tangy pickle, redolent of hot afternoons in India. I like its sharp, zesty flavor and slightly chewy texture. It works well with shrimp curries, roasted chicken, Moroccan tagines, and hard cheeses such as Cheddar or manchego.

Lemon and apricot pickle

⏱ TAKES 35 MINUTES   🍲 MAKES 4LB (1.8KG)   🥫 KEEPS FOR UP TO 1 YEAR

1 Squeeze the juice from the lemons and reserve. Using a food processor or a knife, finely dice the lemon shells, onions, and apricots. If using a processor, do this in batches. Blend or process the garlic, ginger, and chiles to a paste. Alternatively, use a mortar and pestle.

2 Put all the ingredients, including the reserved lemon juice, in a large nonreactive pot, and warm over medium heat. Once the sugar has dissolved, bring the mixture to a boil and simmer for 30 minutes until it thickens.

3 Ladle into hot sterilized jars, cover with vinegar-proof seals, and label.

VARIATION
The mustard seeds make this pickle quite spicy, so for a milder taste replace them with crushed nigella seed. Nigella seed is also known variously as black onion seed, black caraway seed, or kalonji.

INGREDIENTS

1lb 2oz (500g) lemons

1lb 2oz (500g) large onions, chopped

9oz (250g) dried apricots

8–10 garlic cloves

1¾oz (50g) fresh root ginger

2–4 red chiles, seeded if desired

14oz (400g) Demerara or raw sugar

2 tbsp black or brown mustard seeds

2 tbsp salt

2 cups white wine vinegar

Limoncello is a very sweet lemon liqueur that comes from the south of Italy near Sorrento. There, wonderful lemons with thick fragrant peel are steeped in alcohol, then sweetened with the addition of a sugar syrup. I have simplified the process in my recipe.

Limoncello vodka

🕐 NO COOKING   🍲 MAKES 4 CUPS   🥫 KEEPS FOR UP TO 1 YEAR

1 Begin by carefully peeling or grating all the yellow peel from the outside of the lemons. Take care not to include any of the white pith. I find a Microplane grater does this in the most efficient way.

2 Combine the vodka and lemon peel in a glass bowl, cover with plastic wrap, and leave for 30 days in a cool, dark place.

3 Add the sugar and stir daily, covering the mixture again each time, until the sugar has completely dissolved.

4 Strain and discard the lemon peel. Bottle the liqueur, seal, and label. Store in the freezer, and serve well chilled.

INGREDIENTS

8 preferably unwaxed lemons, scrubbed

4 cups (1 liter) vodka

9oz (250g) granulated sugar

Sour oranges rather than sweet ones are the basis for this recipe, because it is the peel that's needed here. Rinse the oranges thoroughly and remove all the white pith. Chopped before use, the condiment adds a lovely fragrance to Chinese cooking, game dishes, and tagines.

Salt-cured oranges

🕐 NO COOKING   🍲 MAKES 1LB 10OZ (750G)   🥫 KEEPS FOR 1 YEAR

1 Pack the oranges into glass jars, sprinkling with salt as you layer them. When the jars are full, add enough water to cover the fruit completely. Label the jars and secure the lids, then shake gently.

2 Look to see that there is still salt visible in each jar. If you can't see a layer of white salt, add more and keep on adding until the solution is saturated. Press the fruit under the liquid, and store in a cool, dark place, shaking the jars and topping off with salt from time to time. Store for about 6 weeks before using.

INGREDIENTS

4–6 Seville or other bitter sour oranges, scrubbed and quartered

9oz (250g) coarse sea salt, plus extra as needed

Jars of preserved lemons are a must-have ingredient these days. They look gorgeous and are simple to make. The down side? Well, you have to wait a few months before they're ready to use. Pack them into jars with glass lids to prevent the lids becoming corroded by salt. To use, scrape away the pith, finely chop the rind, and add to sauces, mashed potatoes, and tagines.

Preserved lemons

○ NO COOKING   🍲 MAKES 2¼LB (1KG)   🗄 KEEPS FOR UP TO 2 YEARS

1 Scrub the lemons under hot water. Cut the lemons into quarters, leaving them attached at the base. Pack these tightly into jars, adding a generous layer of salt between each layer of fruit. Push the lemons down well, then fill the jars with water. Put the lids on, then gently shake each jar. If all the salt dissolves, open the jar and add more.

2 Repeat the process each day for two weeks, gently shaking each jar and adding more salt if necessary. You must always be able to see a layer of salt sitting in the bottom of the jars. If you want the preserved lemons to look even prettier, tuck a couple of bay leaves and a chile down the sides as you layer.

3 Store in a cool, dark place. Let stand for 3 months before using.

INGREDIENTS

2¼lb (1kg) lemons, preferably unwaxed

9oz (250g) cooking salt, plus extra as needed

bay leaves, for garnish (optional)

whole chiles, for garnish (optional)

USING THE PITH AND BRINE

I use the normally discarded flesh and salty liquid from preserved lemons to season white fish such as cod, haddock, or pollock. Spread the pith and a few spoonfuls of liquid over the fish; marinate for 1–2 hours, then rinse, pat dry, and cook.

Index

Page numbers in *italic* refer to the illustrations

A
acidity 15
apples 114–15, *114–15*
  apple butter 113
  apple, plum, and onion relish
    124, *125*
  blackberry and apple jam
    148, *149*
  bramble jelly 151
  cardamom and pineapple
    conserve 170
  chunky apple sauce 126
  cinnamon apple jelly 116, *117*
  crab apple jelly 112
  curried apple and date chutney
    127
  dried fruit and apple chutney
    128, 129
  easy apple and onion chutney
    127
  garlic and green chile jelly 184
  ginger jelly 185
  green tomato chutney 90, *91*
  lavender jelly *136*, 137
  lemongrass and chile jelly 184
  pear, apple, and ginger conserve
    112
  pear, apple, and tomato chutney
    126
  rosemary jelly 135
  rowan jelly 160
  scented geranium leaf jelly 134
 apricots: apricot and lime jam
    54
  apricot and red onion relish 69
  apricot jam 52, *53*
  lemon and apricot pickle 214

B
balsamic vinegar, pickled garlic in 93
banana relish 178
barbecue sauce 192
basil *139*
bay leaves *138*
beet: beet and orange
  relish 92
  pickled beets 103
berries 24–49, 152
  berry vinegar 47
  jumbleberry jam 26, *27*
  pectin 30–31
  see also raspberries,
    strawberries *etc.*

best-ever raspberry jam *34*, 35
black cherry preserve 38
blackberries 31, *153*
  berry vinegar 47
  blackberry and apple jam
    148, *149*
  blackberry jam 28
  blackberry vodka 48
  bramble jelly 151
  wild berry jam 150
black currants 30, *30*
  berry vinegar 47
  black currant jam 33
blueberries 31, *31*
  blueberry preserve *40*, 41
boiling: jam-making 16
  jellies 18
boysenberries 30
bramble jelly 151
brandy: peaches in brandy 66, 67
  prunes in brandy 65
bread and butter pickle *98*, 99
brining pickles 23

C
cabbage: chow chow 100
  pickled red cabbage *104*, 105
candied chestnuts 156
cardamom: cardamom and
  pineapple conserve 170
  carrot and cardamom jam
    80, 81
carrots: carrot and cardamom jam
  80, 81
  curried cauliflower and carrot
    pickle 101
cauliflower: curried cauliflower and
  carrot pickle 101
cellophane covers 11, *11*
chermoula 189
cherries: black cherry preserve 38
  Morello cherry jam 39
cherry tomato and onion
  relish 87
chestnuts, candied 156
chiles 186–7, *186–7*
  chile, peanut, and garlic
    sauce 196
  chile pepper vodka 197
  corn and chile relish *190*, 191
  eggplant, orange, and coriander
    chutney 82
  garlic and green chile jelly 184
  green tomato chutney 90, *91*
  harissa 189
  lemongrass and chile jelly 184

mango and chile jam 167
nectarine and sweetcorn
  relish 68
red pepper and chile jam 185
red pepper jelly 182, *183*
sweet and sour pickled figs 196
sweet chile dipping sauce
  194, *195*
sweet chile pickled shallots 106
Chinese plum sauce 70, 71
chow chow 100
chutneys 20–2
  chunky zucchini 83
  curried apple and date 127
  easy apple and onion 127
  eggplant, orange, and
    coriander 82
  green tomato 90, *91*
  mango 176, *177*
  peach and ginger 68
  pear, apple, and tomato 126
  potting 13
  red plum, lime, and coriander 73
  storecupboard *128*, 129
  tomato and tamarind 188
cider vinegar 21
cinnamon: cinnamon apple jelly
  116, *117*
  red plum and cinnamon jam
    56, *57*
citrus fruit 200–17
clementine marmalade 211
cloudberry jam 150
conserves: cardamom and
  pineapple 170
  melon and vanilla 164, *165*
  nectarine 64
  pear, apple, and ginger 112
containers 11, *11*
cordials 19
  elderflower 144
  hypocras 179
corn and chile relish *190*, 191
covers 11, *11*
crab apple jelly 112
cranberries 30
  cranberry and orange preserve
    33
  cranberry jelly 44, 45
  frozen cranberry vodka 47
cucumbers: bread and butter pickle
  98, 99
curried apple and date chutney 127
curried cauliflower and carrot
  pickle 101

D

damsons 58, *59*
  damson cheese 55
dates: curried apple and date
    chutney 127
dried fruit: mango chutney 176, *177*
    dried fruit and apple chutney
    128, 129
    peach and ginger chutney 68
drinks 19
  blackberry vodka 48
  chile pepper vodka 197
  elderflower cordial 144
  frozen cranberry vodka 47
  hypocras 179
  limoncello vodka 215
  passion fruit gin 179
  raspberry gin 48, *49*
  sloe gin *158*, 159
dry-salting pickles 23

E

eggplant, orange, and coriander
  chutney 82
elderberries: wild berry jam 150
elderflowers 152
  elderflower cordial 144
equipment 10–11, *10–11*

F

figs: fig jam *120*, 121
  green fig preserve 119
  sweet and sour pickled figs 196
flake test 17
flowers 130–45
frozen cranberry vodka 47
fruit 14
  jam-making 16
  jellies 18
  savory preserves 20
fruit butters 19
  apple 113
  spiced pumpkin 76, 77
fruit cheeses 19
  damson 55
  quince 122, *123*
fruit curds 19
  lemon 211
  orange and lime 212, 213
  raspberry 36, *37*
fruit vinegars 19, 23
  berry 47
  tarragon 142, *143*
funnels 10

G

garlic: chile, peanut, and garlic
  sauce 196
  garlic and green chile jelly 184
  pickled garlic in balsamic vinegar 93

  pickled green beans with garlic
    106
  sweet chile pickled shallots 106
geranium leaves *139*
  scented geranium leaf jelly 134
gherkins, pickled 107
gin: passion fruit gin 179
  raspberry gin 48, 49
  sloe gin *158*, 159
ginger: ginger jelly 185
  orange and ginger marmalade
    202, 203
  peach and ginger chutney 68
  pear, apple, and ginger conserve
    112
  pink pickled ginger *198*, 199
  zucchini and ginger jam 78
gooseberries 30
  gooseberry jam 32
grape jelly 42
grapefruit: pink grapefruit
  marmalade *206*, 207
graters 10
green beans: pickled green beans
  with garlic 106
green fig preserve 119
green tea and lime jelly 141
green tomato chutney 90, *91*
greengages 58, *58*
  greengage jam *60*, 61

H

harissa 189
heat processing 13
herbs 130–45
  sweet herb sugars 140
  see also rosemary, sage *etc.*
honey: orange and honey mustard
  sauce 193
horseradish 152
  horseradish in vinegar 161
hypocras 179

J

jam-making 16–17
  ingredients 14–15
  microwaving 13
  potting 12
jams: apricot 52, *53*
  apricot and lime 54
  best-ever raspberry *34*, 35
  blackberry 28
  blackberry and apple 148, *149*
  black currant 33
  carrot and cardamom *80*, 81
  cloudberry 150
  fig *120*, 121
  gooseberry 32
  greengage *60*, 61
  jumbleberry 26, 27

kiwi fruit 167
loganberry 32
mango and chile 167
Morello cherry 39
red pepper and chile 185
red plum and cinnamon 56, *57*
strawberry, rhubarb, and
  vanilla 29
wild berry 150
zucchini and ginger 78
jars 11, *11*
  filling 12–13
jellies 18
  bramble 151
  cinnamon apple 116, *117*
  crab apple 112
  cranberry *44*, 45
  garlic and green chile 184
  ginger 185
  grape 42
  green tea and lime 141
  lavender *136*, 137
  lemongrass and chile 184
  medlar 118
  mint 140
  mirabelle 65
  passion fruit 171
  peach and red currant 64
  pomegranate 171
  port wine and orange 42
  raspberry 46
  red pepper 182, *183*
  red currant 46
  rosé wine and rose petal 132,
    133
  rose hip 151
  rosemary 135
  rowan 160
  sage and Sauternes 134
  scented geranium leaf 134
  Shiraz wine 43
  sloe gin and juniper 160
jelly bags 10
jumbleberry jam 26, 27
juniper berries: sloe gin and juniper
  jelly 160

K

ketchup: spicy plum 72
  tomato 88, 89
ketjap manis 193
kiwi fruit *169*
  kiwi fruit jam 167
kumquat marmalade 210

L

labeling jars 13
lavender *138*
  lavender jelly *136*, 137
lemon 15, 208–9, 208–9

elderflower cordial 144
lemon and apricot pickle 214
lemon curd 211
lemon marmalade 204
limoncello vodka 215
mint jelly 140
preserved lemons 216, 217
lemongrass 139
lemongrass and chile jelly 184
pears in white wine with
lemongrass 110, 111
lids 11, 11
limes 208–9
apricot and lime jam 54
elderflower cordial 144
green tea and lime jelly 141
lime jelly marmalade 210
mango, passion fruit, and lime
preserve 166
orange and lime curd 212, 213
red plum, lime and coriander
chutney 73
limoncello vodka 215
liqueurs: blackberry vodka 48
chile pepper vodka 197
frozen cranberry vodka 47
limoncello vodka 215
passion fruit gin 179
raspberry gin 48, 49
sloe gin 158, 159
loganberries 30
loganberry jam 32

M
malt vinegar 21
mangoes 169
mango and chile jam 167
mango chutney 176, 177
mango, passion fruit, and lime
preserve 166
marmalade: clementine 211
easy everyday 205
kumquat 210
lemon 204
lime jelly 210
orange and ginger 202, 203
pink grapefruit 206, 207
rhubarb 79
whisky 205
measuring equipment 10
medlar jelly 118
melons 168
melon and vanilla conserve
164, 165
microwaving jam 13
mint 139
mint jelly 140
mirabelles 58, 58
mirabelle jelly 65
mirin: teriyaki sauce 194

Morello cherry jam 39
mushrooms: pickled mushrooms
102
mustard: orange and honey
mustard sauce 193

N
nasturtium berries, pickled 145
nectarines: nectarine and
sweetcorn relish 68
nectarine conserve 64
nectarines in brandy 67
nuts 152

O
onions: apple, plum, and onion
relish 124, 125
apricot and red onion relish 69
cherry tomato and onion
relish 87
Chinese plum sauce 70, 71
chow chow 100
chunky zucchini chutney 83
curried apple and date
chutney 127
easy apple and onion
chutney 127
green tomato chutney 90, 91
lemon and apricot pickle 214
onion marmalade 93
pickled onions 94, 95
pineapple and red onion relish
172, 173
oranges 208–9, 209
beet and orange relish 92
easy everyday marmalade 205
eggplant, orange, and coriander
chutney 82
elderflower cordial 144
orange and ginger marmalade
202, 203
orange and honey mustard
sauce 193
orange and lime curd 212, 213
port wine and orange jelly 42
rhubarb marmalade 79
salt-cured oranges 215
whisky marmalade 205
orchard fruits 108–29

P
pans 10
passion fruit 169
mango, passion fruit, and lime
preserve 166
passion fruit gin 179
passion fruit jelly 171
peaches: peach and ginger
chutney 68
peach and pistachio preserve

62, 63
peach and red currant jelly 64
peaches in brandy 66, 67
peanut butter: chile, peanut, and
garlic sauce 196
pears: pear, apple, and ginger
conserve 112
pear, apple, and tomato
chutney 126
pears in white wine with
lemongrass 110, 111
pectin 15, 30–31, 208
peppers 186, 187
bread and butter pickle 98, 99
chow chow 100
pickled sweet peppers 197
red pepper and chile jam 185
red pepper jelly 182, 183
piccalilli 96
pickles 21, 23
beet 103
bread and butter pickle 98, 99
chow chow 100
curried cauliflower and
carrot 101
garlic in balsamic vinegar 93
gherkins 107
green beans with garlic 106
horseradish in vinegar 161
lemon and apricot 214
mushrooms 102
nasturtium berries 145
onions 94, 95
piccalilli 96
pink pickled ginger 198, 199
ploughman's pickle 97
red cabbage 104, 105
samphire 161
sweet and sour pickled figs 196
sweet peppers 197
walnuts 157
watermelon rind pickle 175
pineapple 169
cardamom and pineapple
conserve 170
pineapple and red onion relish
172, 173
pink grapefruit marmalade 206, 207
pink pickled ginger 198, 199
pistachio nuts: peach and pistachio
preserve 62, 63
ploughman's pickle 97
plums 58–9, 58–9
apple, plum, and onion relish 124,
125
Chinese plum sauce 70, 71
mirabelle jelly 65
red plum and cinnamon jam 56,
57
red plum, lime and coriander

chutney 73
spicy plum ketchup 72
wild berry jam 150
pomegranate jelly 171
port wine and orange jelly 42
potting jams and chutneys 12–13
preserves: black cherry 38
blueberry 40, 41
cranberry and orange 33
green fig 119
mango, passion fruit, and
lime 166
peach and pistachio 62, 63
Sue's strawberry 28
sweet watermelon 174
preserving pans 10
prunes in brandy 65
pumpkin butter, spiced 76, 77

Q
quince cheese 122, 123

R
raspberries 30, 31
berry vinegar 47
best-ever raspberry jam 34, 35
raspberry curd 36, 37
raspberry gin 48, 49
raspberry jelly 46
red cabbage, pickled 104, 105
red pepper and chile jam 185
red pepper jelly 182, 183
red plum and cinnamon jam 56, 57
red plum, lime and coriander
chutney 73
red currants 30, 30
peach and red currant jelly 64
red currant jelly 46
relishes 20–2
apple, plum, and onion 124, 125
apricot and red onion 69
beet and orange 92
cherry tomato and onion 87
corn and chile 190, 191
fresh banana 178
nectarine and sweetcorn 68
onion marmalade 93
pineapple and red onion
172, 173
tomato and fennel hamburger
relish 86
rhubarb: rhubarb marmalade 79
strawberry, rhubarb, and vanilla
jam 29
rice wine vinegar 21
rose petals 138
rosé wine and rose petal jelly
132, 133
rose hips 152
rose hip jelly 151

rose hip syrup 154, 155
rosemary 138
rosemary jelly 135
rowan berries 153
rowan jelly 160
rubber rings 11, 11

S
sage 139
sage and Sauternes jelly 134
salt: pickles 23
preserved lemons 216, 217
salt-cured oranges 215
samphire 152
pickled samphire 161
sauces: chile, peanut, and garlic 196
Chinese plum 70, 71
chunky apple 126
harissa 189
ketjap manis 193
orange and honey mustard 193
smoky barbecue 192
sweet chile dipping sauce
194, 195
teriyaki 194
Sauternes: sage and Sauternes
jelly 134
scented geranium leaf jelly 134
set, testing for 16–17, 22
shallots, sweet chile pickled 106
Shiraz wine jelly 43
sieves 10
skimming jam 16
sloes 58
sloe gin 158, 159
sloe gin and juniper jelly 160
smoky barbecue sauce 192
soy sauce: Chinese plum sauce
70, 71
ketjap manis 193
teriyaki sauce 194
spices 21, 180–99
spoons 10
sterilizing jars 11
stone fruit 50–73
storing preserves 13
strawberries 31, 31
strawberry, rhubarb, and vanilla
jam 29
Sue's strawberry preserve 28
sugar 14, 20
sweet herb sugars 140
sultanas: chunky zucchini
chutney 83
green tomato chutney 90, 91
sweet and sour pickled figs 196
sweet chile dipping sauce 194, 195
sweet chile pickled shallots 106
sweet herb sugars 140
sweet watermelon preserve 174

sweetcorn: corn and chile relish
190, 191
nectarine and sweetcorn
relish 68
syrup, rose hip 154, 155

T
tamarind: tomato and tamarind
chutney 188
tarragon vinegar 142, 143
tayberries 30
tea: green tea and lime jelly 141
techniques 8–23
teriyaki sauce 194
thyme 139
tomatoes 84–5, 84–5
cherry tomato and onion relish
87
green tomato chutney 90, 91
pear, apple, and tomato chutney
126
smoky barbecue sauce 192
tomato and fennel hamburger
relish 86
tomato and tamarind chutney
188
tomato ketchup 88, 89
tropical fruit 162–79

V
vegetables 14, 20–3, 74–107
piccalilli 96
ploughman's pickle 97
see also peppers, tomatoes etc.
vinegar 21, 23
see also chutneys; fruit vinegars;
pickles; relishes
vodka: blackberry vodka 48
chile pepper vodka 197
frozen cranberry vodka 47
limoncello vodka 215

W
walnuts, pickled 157
watermelon 168
sweet watermelon preserve 174
watermelon rind pickle 175
whisky marmalade 205
white currants 30, 30
wild berry jam 150
wild food 146–61
wine: pears in white wine with
lemongrass 110, 111
port wine and orange jelly 42
rosé wine and rose petal jelly
132, 133
sage and Sauternes jelly 134
Shiraz wine jelly 43
wine vinegar 21
wrinkle test 17

Acknowledgments

AUTHOR'S ACKNOWLEDGMENTS

Thank you to everyone involved with this lovely book. The pictures are beautiful and the editing a work of much patience and commitment, so my thanks go to Jean Cazals and Diana Craig, respectively. I was fortunate once again to have the unstinting support of my husband, Bob, and daughters, Jade and Amber, who proved committed critics and who washed up. Often. Dr. Colin May, adviser to Certo Ltd,. provided me with much learned correspondence on the subject of pectin, and I thank him for his patience as he helped me both to understand and to learn to love this useful substance. Good friends as ever have been supportive and forbearing, so thanks to Susan Flemming, Celia Kent, and Tim Etchells. Finally, my enduring thanks go to my mother, who taught me early of the many things in life that are worth preserving.

PUBLISHER'S ACKNOWLEDGMENTS

Dorling Kindersley would like to thank Valerie Barrett and Katie Rogers for recipe testing; and Hilary Bird for the index.

The publisher would also like to thank the following for their kind permission to reproduce their photographs:
(a-above; b-below/bottom; c-centre; f-far; l-left; r-right; t-top)
14 Kate Whitaker (r); 15 DK Library (l); 15 John Davis (r); 17 William Reavell (br); 20 DK Library (r); 21 Dave King (l); 21 Hugh Johnson (r)